Securing a Level 3
Mathematics
Teacher's Book

Hilary Koll and Steve Mills

Rising Stars UK Ltd.
22 Grafton Street, London W1S 4EX
www.risingstars-uk.com

Every effort has been made to trace copyright holders and obtain their permission
for the use of copyright materials. The authors and publisher will gladly receive
information enabling them to rectify any error or omission in subsequent editions.

All facts are correct at time of going to press.

Text, design and layout © Rising Stars UK Ltd.

The right of Hilary Koll and Steve Mills to be identified as the authors of this work
has been asserted by them in accordance with the Copyright, Design and Patents Act
1998.

Published 2010

Authors: Hilary Koll and Steve Mills
Consultant Maths Publisher: Jean Carnall
Text design: Laura de Grasse
Typesetting: Ray Rich
Artwork: David Woodroffe
Cover Design: Burville-Riley Partnership

All rights reserved. No part of this publication may be reproduced, stored in a
retrieval system, or transmitted, in any form by any means, electronic, mechanical,
photocopying, recording or otherwise, without the prior permission of Rising Stars.

British Library Cataloguing in Publication Data.
A CIP record for this book is available from the British Library.

ISBN: 978-1-84680-719-0

Printed by Ashford Colour Press

Contents

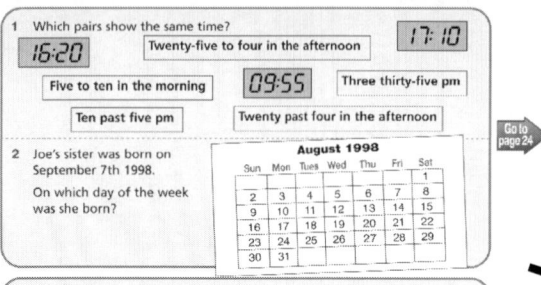

Unit 3 – System scan

1 Which pairs show the same time?

16:20 | Twenty-five to four in the afternoon | 17:10

Five to ten in the morning | 09:55 | Three thirty-five pm

Ten past five pm | Twenty past four in the afternoon

Go to page 24

2 Joe's sister was born on September 7th 1998.
On which day of the week was she born?

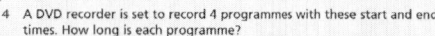

August 1998

Sun	Mon	Tues	Wed	Thu	Fri	Sat
						1
2	3	4	5	6	7	8
9	10	11	12	13	14	15
16	17	18	19	20	21	22
23	24	25	26	27	28	29
30	31					

3 Which numbers are missing?

a   140 secs = 2 mins and ☐ secs   b   3 weeks = ☐ days
c   250 mins = ☐ hours and ☐ mins   d   4 years = ☐ months
e   1½ days = ☐ hours   f   2 hours and 25 mins = ☐ mins

Go to page 26

4 A DVD recorder is set to record 4 programmes with these start and end times. How long is each programme?

START END   START END
2:45 PM 3:17 PM   1:36 PM 4:05 PM
7:19 AM 9:04 AM   9:48 PM 0:29 AM

Go to page 28

5 Marco buys a book and a sunhat for £5.17.
a   What is the cost of the book?
b   How much change does he get from £20?

£3.29

Go to page 30

6 Safia buys 5 bananas, 1 melon and 3 pineapples.
Use a calculator to find the total cost.

36p each
£2.17 each
£1.99 each

Go to page 32

7

1

Review and Assess

Written and mental questions help teachers identify what pupils know, where there are gaps in their knowledge and to highlight misconceptions.

Check-up scan 3A   Name: _____

1 Write an addition and two multiplications for the number of spots on the ladybirds on each of these leaves.

a   b

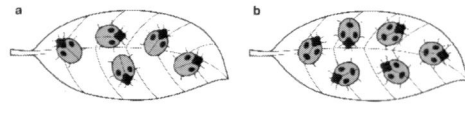

_____   _____
_____   _____
_____   _____

2 Write a multiplication to show how each of these additions could be written.

a   4 + 4 + 4 + 4 + 4 + 4 + 4 = 28 _____

b   6 + 6 + 6 + 6 + 6 = 30 _____

c   3 + 3 + 3 + 3 + 3 + 3 + 3 = 21 _____

3 Use the fact in the box to help you answer each of the questions.

$5 \times 8 = 40$

a   There are 8 chocolate bars in a pack. How many bars in 5 packs? ____

b   A school organises 40 children into 5 teams. How many children in each team? ____

c   A packet of crisps costs 40p. How much does it cost to buy 8 packets? ____

Train your brain!

__ × __ = 24

Write as many multiplication facts with the answer 24 as you can.

I can show repeated addition as multiplication.   ☐
I can solve problems that involve multiplication.   ☐

5

Review and Assess

Review learning and ask the pupils to complete the Check-up scan. This helps them check they're confident with all aspects of the key objectives covered.

pproach
a level

2

ach

the clear teachers notes
elp you address the gaps
g a range of activities
uding, mental maths
stions, opportunities to
about mathematics
hands-on
vities.

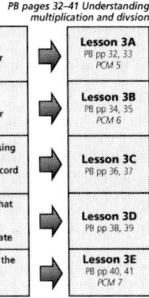

Unit 3 Understanding and using multiplication and division

Objectives

PB pages 32–41 Understanding
multiplication and division

• recognise when situations involving repeated addition are more efficiently represented using multiplication • use known facts to work out related ones, for example, use 3 × 4 = 12 to answer 30 × 4 or 120 ÷ 40	**Lesson 3A** PB pp 32, 33 PCM 5
• recognise when situations involving equal sharing or grouping or repeated subtraction are more efficiently represented using division • use known facts to work out related ones, for example, use 3 × 4 = 12 to answer 30 × 4 or 120 ÷ 40	**Lesson 3B** PB pp 34, 35 PCM 6
• represent arrays using multiplication and carry out multiplication calculations using arrays • use partitioning to multiply a two-digit number by a single-digit number and record steps	**Lesson 3C** PB pp 36, 37
• interpret division as the inverse of multiplication, for example, understanding that 24 ÷ 4 can be found using 4 × 6 = 24 • divide a two-digit by a single-digit number by splitting it into sensible chunks • find and interpret remainders in division, rounding up or down where appropriate	**Lesson 3D** PB pp 38, 39
• find a unit fraction, for example, 1/5 of an amount using division, then multiply the answer to find non-unit fractions, for example, 2/5, 3/5	**Lesson 3E** PB pp 40, 41 PCM 7

Key vocabulary

digit, place value, number, numeral, position, units/ones, tens, hundreds, number lines, multiple, multiply, divide, share, product, times, groups of, lots of, equal groups, counting on, counting back, number sentence, recall, method, chunking, array

Teaching resources, ideas and mental starters

ITP software, squared paper, arrays, cubes, counters, counting equipment, bricks, base 10 materials, bead strings, number lines

Counting sticks and number lines can be used to count on and back in equal steps to and from zero.

Bead strings for dividing and arrays

Review and access prior learning

Errors and misconceptions – System scan 3

1. Assist children with the first addition and multiplication, e.g. 3 + 3 + 3 + 3 and 5 × 3. Then note whether they can apply these ideas to find another multiplication and do the same for the next set. Observe whether the child resorts to counting spots to find the answers or whether counting on or tables facts are used.
2. Provide counting equipment if necessary. Encourage children to explain how they worked out each answer. Observe whether they share out objects, use known tables facts or whether they use some other method.
3. Does the child understand multiplication as an array? Can they use this idea more abstractly to work out the answer to 4 × 26? Provide further questions of this type to assess this in more detail if necessary.
4. Observe whether the child uses a chunking method or a different approach. Do they understand remainders and record them appropriately?
5, 6 Is the child able to find a unit fraction (numerator 1) of a number? Is division used? Observe whether practical materials are needed or whether knowledge of tables facts is secure and drawn upon

---

g multiplication

PB pp 32 & 33

in activity, revising counting on in equal steps from zero. Note which
with and use a counting stick to practise those more difficult multiples to

repeated addition and multiplication by looking together at the **Power up**
describe the multiplications, e.g. 4 times 3 or 4 multiplied by 4, or 4 lots of 3.
children to read the facts aloud. Ensure that children understand the × sign and
to notice that 4 × 5 can represent 4 lots of 5 spots or 4 spots multiplied by 5.
same answer.

to become more confident with understanding the link between repeated
provide pupils in each pair with a copy of the cards on PCM 5. Encourage
om activity and identify how 5 × 7 could be 5 lots of 7 spots or 7 lots of 5

Explore activity. Some children may try answering the questions without
to see the link between each question and the given fact and ask them to
e less on answering the questions and more on understanding how facts
e support in appreciating the link between multiplication and division

ion

PB pp 34 & 35

steps of 5 from 50 and steps of 10 from 100 before asking
allow children time in pairs to look at the **Chat room** activity and
en sorting into groups of 7 or sorting into 7 groups. Explain that both

ctise and encourage them to sort into groups of the given size and
at the answers are the same. Draw attention to which way each child

PCM 6. Children arrange the cards to make true statements and
statement using numbers and the division sign.

activity. Some children may try answering the questions without
link between each question and the given fact and ask them to
answering the questions and more on understanding how facts
rt in appreciating the link between multiplication and division

---

Practise

Practice questions, games
and activities give pupils
lots of opportunities to
gain confidence in key areas.

3

Using multiplication strategies

 **Plug in**

How quickly can you answer these times-tables questions?

a 5 × 4   b 4 × 2   c 3 × 3   d 7 × 2   e 4 × 4   f 5 × 3   g 6 × 2
h 1 × 8   i 4 × 6   j 5 × 0   k 10 × 7   l 5 × 5   m 5 × 9   n 4 × 3

 Power up (1)

The bumps on these building bricks form an **array**.
Write two multiplication facts for each brick.

2 × 4 = 8
4 × 2 = 8

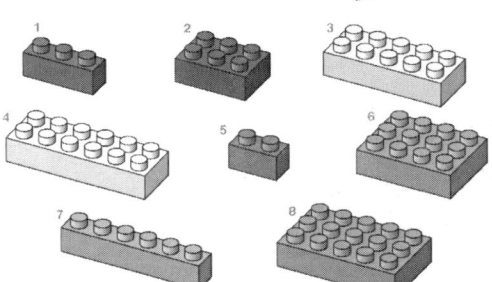

1   2   3
4   5   6
7   8

 **Game play**

1 player

You will need: squared paper and a dice.

• Roll the dice and multiply the two numbers together.
  Record the multiplication fact, e.g. 6 × 4 = 24.
• Draw a rectangle onto squared paper to show the multiplication
  fact as an array and count the squares to check your answer.

36

---

ply

e pupils are
ure in their
wledge and
erstanding, the
lore questions
ble them to utilise
ir skills in different
texts and to solve
thematical
blems.

Understanding multiplication and division (3

 Power up (2)

Find these fractions of the bags of money opposite.

a 3/4 of **A**   b 4/5 of **B**   c 3/5 of **C**   d 2/3 of **D**   e 7/12 of **E**

f 1/4 of **A**   g 4/9 of **B**   h 3/5 of **C**   i 2/9 of **D**   j 5/6 of **E**

 Game play

2+ players

You will need: cards from the top of PCM 7.

• Spread all the cards face down.
• Each player picks a card and finds how many
  gold coins he/she will be given.
• The player with the highest number wins a point.
• The winner is the first player to score 8 points.

 **Explore**

There were 120 sailors on the Goodship Lollipop.
Use division to find the number of sailors:

1/4 were seasick: 120 ÷ 4 = 30 sailors

a 1/6 of sailors had wooden legs.
b 1/12 of sailors were homesick.
c 3/10 of sailors owned a parrot.
d 5/6 of sailors hated the biscuits onboard.
e 1/60 of sailors had eye patches.
f 5/8 of sailors fell overboard.
g 5/12 of sailors owned a cat.
h 1/5 of sailors had scars.
i 7/30 of sailors had walked the plank.

41

4

Unit 1 Understanding the number system

Objectives

PB pages 13–23
Understanding of Numbers

Objectives		Lessons
• read and write numbers that contain zero as a place holder, understanding its role • count in ones and tens, backwards and forwards, over boundaries, e.g. 187, 197, 207 … • identify the important digits to compare and order two or more numbers, e.g. 184 and 275 (hundreds digit), 384 and 392 (tens digit), 407 and 410 (units and tens digits)	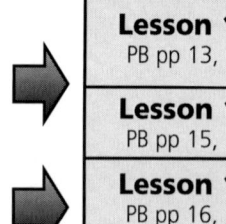	**Lesson 1A** PB pp 13, 14 **Lesson 1B** PB pp 15, 16
• position numbers approximately on partially marked number lines • round a number by identifying the multiple of 10 or 100 to which it is closest		**Lesson 1C** PB pp 16, 17 PCM 1
• compare and order negative and positive numbers, using a number line		**Lesson 1D** PB pp 18, 19
• identify the value of each digit in measures such as grams and in money		**Lesson 1E** PB pp 20, 21
• understand the role of the numerator and denominator of a fraction • identify, read and write fractions to describe a proportion of a shape or amount, e.g. appreciate that, since there are 100 centimetres in a metre, 1 centimetre is equal to 1/100 of a metre		**Lesson 1F** PB pp 22, 23 PCM 2

Key vocabulary

digit, place value, number, numeral, position, units/ones, tens, hundreds, number lines, multiple, round, grams, pounds, pence, measures, numerator, denominator, fraction, positive numbers, negative numbers

Teaching resources, ideas and mental starters

ITP software, calculators, place-value cards, fractional apparatus, follow-me cards, measuring equipment, money

Counting sticks and number lines can be used count on in 10s, 100s and 1000s from any number: for place value work; in any sized steps beyond zero for negative number work; in fractional steps and using measurement (including temperature).

Review and access prior learning

Errors and misconceptions – System scan 1

PART A

1   Provide children with place-value cards, if necessary, for this question. Observe whether children understand that the position of the digit signifies its value.
2   Point out that they must give the number that is one more. Look out for the common error of writing 60 010 for six hundred and ten and observe whether children can correctly count on in ones.
3   Ask children to explain how they compare these numbers and observe whether they understand that the digits to the left are more significant than those to the right.
4, 5 Encourage children to explain their working. Observe whether they understand the movement of digits.
6   Draw attention to which questions are rounding to the nearest 10 and which are to the nearest 100. Observe whether a child knows the convention of rounding those ending in 5 or 50 up to the next 10 or 100, respectively.
7   Does the child correctly identify numbers on the number line? If not, ask them to fill in any numbers they can for the marked positions.

PART B

1   If necessary, allow children to use a number line to help them determine which number in each set is smallest.
2   Does the child incorrectly use £ and p when writing prices, e.g. £0.60p? Is the decimal point correctly placed?
3–5 These questions test children's understanding of decimals used as part of money and measures. Encourage children to read the amounts and measurements aloud to see if they are read correctly and abbreviations known.
6   Observe children's understanding of the role of the numerator and denominator. Do they know to count all the equal parts to find the denominator? Do they know to count the red parts to give the numerator?
7   Does the child know that there are 100 cm in one metre and to write this on the bottom of each fraction?

Unit 1A The value of digits

PB pp 12 & 13

TEACH

Work together to complete the **Plug in** activity, discussing how the numbers change as you count on across boundaries, such as 100s boundaries. Provide further oral counting activities of this type.

Introduce the first **Power up** exercise, providing spellings of the number names to assist pupils. Draw attention to the numbers that involve the digit zero and help children to say and write these, and similar numbers, in words. Encourage children to explain in their own words the purpose of the zero in such numbers, describing how the 0 in 604 distinguished the number from 64. For the second **Power up** activity it can be helpful to show on the board how HTU (or hundreds, tens and ones) can be written above the digits of each number to assist in showing the value of the digits.

PRACTISE

Encourage children, in pairs, to discuss the **Chat room** activity and identify the role of zero in each number. Ask them to say which number is the largest and smallest and to order them. The **Game play** activity helps children to compare and order three-digit numbers. The game can be played in pairs or in a small group. Your own sets of place-value cards could be used for this game, rather than PCM 1, if preferred, although the cards on PCM 1 will create three-digit numbers including zeros. This ensures that children more fully appreciate the role of zero when comparing numbers.

APPLY

The **Explore** puzzle requires children to use clues to identify two- and three-digit numbers. Most children will find the clues for A and H more difficult than the others as they involve crossing the hundreds and tens boundaries. Assist them by asking them to count on in tens or ones respectively.

Unit 1B Multiplying and dividing by 10

PB pp 14 & 15

TEACH

Begin by counting on in tens from zero to 100, holding out another finger each time a number is said. Then ask children to copy and complete the sequence in the **Plug in** activity, explaining that the sequence continues beyond 100, still counting in tens.

Discuss the information in the first **Chat room** activity and encourage pupils to see that there is a movement of the digits, rather than teaching to 'add a nought'. This could be shown practically by moving digit cards across the columns.

PRACTISE

Ask pupils to tackle the **Power up** exercise using what they have learnt from the information box. Similarly discuss the second **Chat room** information box and ask pupils to work together to divide by 10, again emphasising the movement of digits, not the removal of a zero.

The **Game play** activity provides practice in multiplying and dividing by 10 and requires a counter per player and a dice per pair.

APPLY

The **Explore** activity shows a real-life use for multiplying (and dividing) by 10. Once they have completed the activity, encourage children to discuss how multiplying by 10 is related to dividing by 10, showing how the number of millimetres can be divided by 10 to find the number of centimetres.

Unit 1C Number lines and rounding

PB pp 16 & 17

TEACH

Work together to complete the **Plug in** activity, referring to number lines to help children find halfway numbers. Provide further oral questions of this type to reinforce the activity.

The **Power up** exercise begins by considering rounding to the nearest multiple of 10. Discuss the convention of rounding **up** numbers exactly halfway between the multiples of 10 (i.e. those ending in 5). Similarly, as the activity moves on to rounding to the nearest multiple of 100, talk about how numbers exactly halfway between the multiples of 100 (i.e. those ending in 50) round up.

PRACTISE

Encourage children, in pairs, to work together to identify the arrowed numbers in the **Chat room** activity. Ask them to explain how they worked out each number, using clues such as: *It is a bit less than halfway between 90 and 100 so must be about 94.* The **Game play** activity provides opportunity for practice in rounding three-digit numbers. Your own sets of place value cards could be used for this game, rather than PCM 1, if preferred, although the cards on PCM 1 will create three-digit numbers including zeros. This ensures that children more fully appreciate the role of zero when rounding numbers. For further practice of rounding to the nearest 10, children could select place value cards and round them accordingly.

APPLY

Discuss the use of the letter g to stand for grams in the **Explore** problem-solving activity. To extend this activity further, if required, children could write their own descriptions for other masses to swap with friends.

Unit 1D Positive and negative numbers

PB pp 18 & 19

TEACH

Begin by examining the thermometer picture and discussing temperature. Model how to read the negative numbers and ask children to count down below zero. Then ask the children to complete the **Plug in** activity and discuss the answers together.

Look at the information box as part of the **Chat room** activity and ask children to talk to a partner about which of the statements are true and which are false. Ensure that children realise that, although 5 is greater than 4, –5 is less than –4.

PRACTISE

Children can then tackle the problems in the **Power up** exercise, including ordering positive and negative integers. The **Game play** activity helps children to become more familiar with seeing negative numbers on number lines and reading the numbers aloud. Pupils in each pair require a coin (or counter) and two dice. Demonstrate how the two dice are rolled and the total found in the key to tell them how to move the coin. Remind them that 'up' means moving towards larger numbers and 'down' means moving towards smaller (negative) numbers. Ensure that they realise that, to win, they can land on or pass 10 or –10.

APPLY

For the **Explore** activity, children must use the clues to work out the midday temperature each day during one week.

Unit 1E Decimals – money and measures

PB pp 20 & 21

TEACH

Allow children time to copy and complete the sequences of the **Plug in** activity before discussing how the sequences in each pair show the same information, just written in a different way, for the **Chat room** activity. Encourage children to remember that ten 10p coins are the same as a pound, so one tenth of a pound is 10p and, by showing a metre stick, help them to see that one tenth of a metre is 10 cm. Show them that the digit to the right of a dot/decimal point shows how many tenths (of a pound or metre) there are.

PRACTISE

Help children to pursue these relationships further by tackling the **Power up** exercise. When assisting pupils, use the term 'tenths digit' to refer to the digit to the right of the dot and encourage them to make the link between this digit and tenths of a pound/metre. Similarly, the hundredths digit can be introduced as it occurs. Explain that 0.5 m is the same as 0.50 m in the second Power up activity. The **Game play** activity is an individual matching task. Pupils will need coloured cubes (or counters) for this. Discuss the rules and explain that not every colour will require the same number of cubes.

APPLY

Pupils will require a metre stick per pair for the **Explore** activity. Encourage children to measure carefully and record answers both in centimetres and in metres.

Power up: **1a** £0.50 **b** £0.40 **c** 70p **d** £0.80 **e** £0.90 **f** 85p **g** £0.99 **h** £1.00 or £1
2a 70 cm **b** 0.4 m **c** 0.9 m **d** 25 cm **e** 0.65 m **f** 72 cm

Unit 1F Understanding fractions

PB pp 22 & 23

TEACH

Allow children time to complete the **Plug in** activity, encouraging them to say the fractions aloud to ensure they are being described correctly. Point out how the numbers in the fractions are obtained, e.g. 2/5 means that there are 5 equal parts altogether and 2 of them are shaded. Make sure that children appreciate which fractions form set A and which form set B, etc.

Introduce the role of the denominator (bottom number) and numerator (top number) through discussing the **Chat room** activity. Encourage children to remember that they must count **all** the equal parts to find the denominator, not just those coloured or uncoloured.

PRACTISE

Help children to pursue these ideas further by tackling the **Power up** exercise. When assisting pupils, encourage them to start by finding the denominator (the bottom number) by counting up all the parts and then finally counting the number that are coloured to give the numerator. Watch out for children incorrectly giving the denominator as the number of uncoloured parts.

Provide pupils with coloured pencils and a copy of PCM 2 per child (or pair). Once they have coloured and cut out the cards, they can play the **Game play** activity in pairs, which involves comparing fractions. If pupils are unsure or if they think the fractions are equivalent, they can replace the cards and pick again. Discuss any difficulties with the class at the end. Children may have begun to notice that some fractions are equivalent to other fractions they know, e.g. that $\frac{2}{8}$ is the same as $\frac{1}{4}$ or $\frac{3}{6}$ is the same as one half, etc.

APPLY

The **Explore** activity is designed to help children to begin to see that fractions can be used in more abstract contexts, where fractions are not represented as shapes. Encourage children to talk to a partner about their work and to agree answers together. Ask them to describe what they have learnt in the lesson to allow for further consolidation.

Answers
System scans

Unit 1 (PB pp 4–5)

Part A   1a 3 or 3 units/ones **b** 30 or 3 tens **c** 8 or 8 units/ones **d** 700 or 7 hundreds **e** 20 or 2 tens **f** 0 or no units/ones

2a 100 **b** 213 **c** 327 **d** 804 **e** 600 **f** 610 **3a** 634 **b** 920 **c** 747 **d** 333 **e** 487 **f** 505 **4a** 60 **b** 90 **c** 460 **d** 390 **e** 600 **5a** 8 **b** 2 **c** 88 **d** 52 **e** 40 **6a** 70 **b** 500 **c** 170 **d** 500 **e** 440 **f** 300 **7a** 20 **b** 35 **c** 51 **d** 80 **e** 89

Part B   1a –6 **b** –6 **c** –8 **d** –5 **e** –7 **f** –2 **2a** £0.60 **b** £0.75 **c** £1.20 **3** 15 **4** 135 cm **5** 0.3 m or 0.30 m **6a** $\frac{1}{6}$ **b** $\frac{5}{6}$ **c** $\frac{3}{8}$ **d** $\frac{6}{16}$ **7a** $\frac{7}{100}$ m **b** $\frac{43}{100}$ m **c** $\frac{89}{100}$ m

Pupil's Book questions

Unit 1A (PB pp 12–13)

Plug in: 1 95, 96, 97, 98, 99, 100, 101, 102, 103, 104, 105 **2** 170, 180, 190, 200, 210, 220, 230, 240, 250, 260, 270 **3** 445, 455, 465, 475, 485, 495, 505, 515, 525, 535, 545 **4** 677, 687, 697, 707, 717, 727, 737, 747, 757, 767, 777 **5** 403, 413, 423, 433, 443, 453, 463, 473, 483, 493, 503

Power up: 1 ninety-two, eight hundred and ten, three hundred and sixty-one, five hundred and forty, two hundred and five, four hundred and three

Explore: A 708, **B** 457, **C** 657, **D** 648, **E** 407, **F** 640, **G** 650, **H** 710, **I** 10

Unit 1B (PB pp 14–15)

Plug in: 10, 20, 30, 40, 50, 60, 70, 80, 90, 100, 110, 120, 130, 140, 150, 160, 170, 180, 190, 200

Power up: 1a 20 **b** 60 **c** 80 **d** 30 **e** 70 **f** 110 **g** 260 **h** 520

2a 70 **b** 450 **c** 800 **d** 710 **e** 490 **f** 900

Chat room: a 3 **b** 42 **c** 80 **d** 51 **e** 47 **f** 50

Explore: 1 5.1 cm, 51 mm **2** 3.8 cm, 38 mm **3** 6.4 cm, 64 mm

Unit 1C (PB pp 16–17)

Plug in: a 50 **b** 10 **c** 45 **d** 75 **e** 250 **f** 700 **g** 250 **h** 500

Power up: 1a 150 **b** 170 **c** 150 **d** 170 **e** 160 **f** 180 **2** 170 **3a** 260 **b** 380 **c** 420 **d** 800 **e** 300 **f** 110 **4a** 700 **b** 600 **c** 900 **d** 500 **e** 900 **f** 100

Chat room: a 10 **b** 25 **c** 49 **d** 70 **e** 94 **f** 100 **g** 200 **h** 450 **i** about 620 **j** about 890

Explore: 1 D **2** C **3** E **4** B **5** A

Unit 1D (PB pp 18–19)

Plug in: a –1 °C **b** –5 °C **c** –3 °C **d** –6 °C **e** –7 °C **f** –8 °C

Power up: 1 –9, –6, –2, 4, 8 **2** –10, –6, –2, 0, 3, 8

Explore: Mon 3 °C, Tue 1 °C, Wed –2 °C, Thur –4 °C, Fri –6 °C, Sat –3 °C, Sun –2 °C

Unit 1E (PB pp 20–21)

Plug in: a 10p, 20p, 30p, 40p, 50p, 60p, 70p, 80p, 90p, 100p
b £0.10, £0.20, £0.30, £0.40, £0.50, £0.60, £0.70, £0.80, £0.90, £1.00
c 10 cm, 20 cm, 30 cm, 40 cm, 50 cm, 60 cm, 70 cm, 80 cm, 90 cm, 100 cm
d 0.1 m, 0.2 m, 0.3 m, 0.4 m, 0.5 m, 0.6 m, 0.7 m, 0.8 m, 0.9 m, 1.0 m

Power up: 1a £0.50 **b** £0.40 **c** 70p **d** £0.80 **e** £0.90 **f** 85p **g** £0.99 **h** £1.00 or £1 **2a** 70 cm **b** 0.4 m **c** 0.9 m **d** 25 m **e** 0.65 m **f** 72 cm

Unit 1F (PB pp 22–23)

Plug in: Set A: $\frac{1}{4}, \frac{2}{5}, \frac{3}{4}$ **Set B:** $\frac{1}{5}, \frac{1}{3}, \frac{3}{5}$ **Set C:** $\frac{1}{4}, \frac{1}{2}, \frac{4}{5}$ **Set D:** $\frac{1}{2}, \frac{3}{5}, \frac{2}{3}$

Chat room: $\frac{8}{10}$ (8 out of 10 squares are coloured brown)

Power up: 1 $\frac{3}{4}$ **2** $\frac{10}{12}$ **3** $\frac{1}{6}$ **4** $\frac{3}{6}$ **5** $\frac{7}{12}$ **6** $\frac{5}{9}$ **7** $\frac{5}{10}$ **8** $\frac{1}{9}$ **9** $\frac{2}{5}$

Explore: 1a $\frac{1}{100}$ **b** $\frac{3}{100}$ **c** $\frac{11}{100}$ **d** $\frac{99}{100}$ **2a** $\frac{1}{100}$ **b** $\frac{17}{100}$ **c** $\frac{67}{100}$ **d** $\frac{99}{100}$ **3a** $\frac{1}{1000}$ **b** $\frac{57}{1000}$ **c** $\frac{388}{1000}$ **d** $\frac{750}{1000}$

Check-up scans

1A The value of digits (p52)

1a two hundred and forty pounds **b** eight hundred and five pounds **c** seven hundred and ninety-four pounds

2a 80 **b** 900 **c** 300, 2 **d** 600 **e** 500, 70, 3 **f** 300, 10, 0

3a 455, 465, 475, 485, 495, 505 **b** 7, 107, 207, 307, 407, 507

Train your brain!

0, 7, 8, 70, 78, 80, 87, 708, 780, 807, 870

1B Multiplying and dividing by 10 (p53)

1 No, the answer is 480.

2a 430 **b** 320 **c** 500

3a 70 **b** 120 **c** 600

4 28, 79, 90

Train your brain!

Six true statements:
$24 \times 10 = 240$, $240 \div 10 = 24$, $300 \div 10 = 30$, $30 \div 10 = 3$, $3 \times 10 = 30$, $30 \times 10 = 300$

1C Number lines and rounding (p54)

1a 180 **b** 340 **c** 500 **d** 300 **e** 250 **f** 890

2a 200 **b** 300 **c** 500 **d** 300 **e** 200 **f** 900

3 Check numbers are correctly marked on scale.

4a 9 **b** 27 **c** 49 **d** 74 **e** 82

Train your brain!

345 up to 354 – 10 numbers   450 up to 549 – 100 numbers

1D Positive and negative numbers (p55)

1a –9, –5, –4, 1, 7 **b** –10, –8, –5, –4, –2, –1, 2, 4, 7, 8, 10

2a –3 °C **b** –4 °C **c** –2 °C **d** –7 °C **e** –7 °C **f** –8 °C **g** –6 °C **h** –8 °C

3a –6, –3, –2, 0, 4, 5 **b** –7, –6, –4, –2, 0, 1, 7 **c** –5, –4, –3, –2, 3, 5, 6

1E Decimals money and measures (p56)

1a 40p **b** 69p **c** 258p

2a £0.38 **b** £0.47 **c** £1.48

3 36

4a 100 cm **b** 150 cm **c** 357 cm

5a 0.5 m **b** 2.5 m **c** 1.75 m

6 280 cm

Train your brain!

Check matching measurements.

1F Understanding fractions (p57)

1a $\frac{1}{4}$ **b** $\frac{5}{6}$ **c** $\frac{7}{10}$ **d** $\frac{4}{5}$ **e** $\frac{5}{9}$ **f** $\frac{7}{12}$

2a $\frac{47}{100}$ **b** $\frac{50}{100}$ or $\frac{1}{2}$

Securing mental addition and subtraction

Objectives

PB pages 24–31 Mental addition and subtraction

Objectives	Lesson
• use known facts to work out related ones, for example, use 7 + 8 = 15 to work out 37 + 8 and 150 – 80	**Lesson 2A** PB pp 24, 25
• partition two-digit numbers to support efficient calculation, for example, 41 – 19 = 21 + 20 – 19 • draw their own number lines to show steps in a calculation • use the inverse operation to check answers, particularly for subtraction, for example, check 56 – 18 = 38 using 38 + 18	**Lesson 2B** PB pp 26, 27 PCM 3
• identify the appropriate calculation(s) needed to solve a problem	**Lesson 2C** PB pp 28, 29 PCM 4
• consider the numbers involved in a particular calculation to make appropriate decisions on which mental method to choose • work out subtraction by counting backwards and by counting forwards and decide which is the more efficient method for particular calculations • use correct mathematical vocabulary to describe/explain their calculation methods	**Lesson 2D** PB pp 30, 31

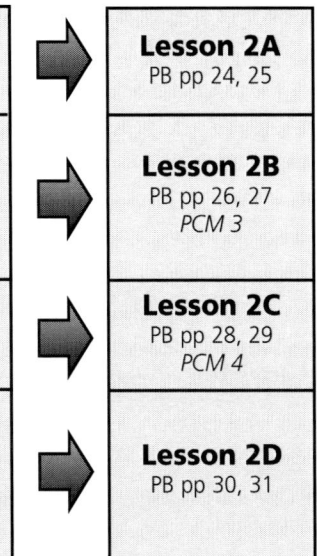

Key vocabulary

digit, number, numeral, units/ones, tens, hundreds, number lines, addition, subtraction, more, less, total, difference, sum, take away, minus, method, counting on, counting back, strategy, problem, number sentence, missing number, partitioning, multiple, inverse

Teaching resources, ideas and mental starters

ITP number line software, bead strings, pegs on a line, addition and subtraction spreadsheets, number lines, digit cards, counting equipment

Number lines, such as those shown below, can be used for demonstrating different methods for solving the same problem, e.g. finding a difference by counting on from the smaller to the larger number or counting back from the larger to the smaller.

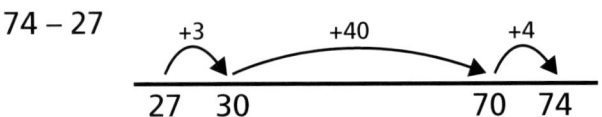

Addition and subtraction grids, as shown here.

+	3	9	5	7
8				
6				

–	3	8	9	6
11				
13				

Review and access prior learning

Errors and misconceptions – System scan 2

1   Observe whether children use the given fact to help them answer each question. Ask them to explain how each fact is related to the one in the blue box.
2   Children may initially need help in knowing what to do. If this is the case, provide the example 4 + 2 = 6 and say that this is related to the following facts: 2 + 4 = 6, 6 – 2 = 4 and 6 – 4 = 2. Then encourage them to attempt the question again.
3   Assist children in reading each problem and observe whether they are able to write an appropriate number sentence for each problem. Note that several different sentences may be appropriate. Encourage children to explain their choices. Note whether the child can correctly perform the calculation, e.g. 100 – 22 = 78, or whether recall of number facts to 20 needs to be improved further.
4   Ask children to tackle the two additions first and observe the strategies used to solve them. Does the child partition the numbers or use a number line in some way? Note whether the child appears to have an understanding of the value of the digits or whether further place value work may be necessary. For the subtraction questions, note whether mistakes are made in subtracting the smaller from the larger, e.g. for the units digits does the child subtract 1 from 4 rather than subtracting 4 from 1 (or 11). Has the child an understanding of subtracting 20 and adjusting when subtracting 19? Note the strategy used for each question. Provide appropriate resources for children to use, e.g. number lines, digit cards, counting equipment.

Unit 2A Using known facts to find others PB pp 24 & 25

TEACH

Encourage children to warm up by testing their knowledge of number bonds in the **Plug in** activity, discussing which facts they find most difficult.

Demonstrate how a fact such as 3 + 4 = 7 can be helpful in finding 30 + 40, and provide pupils with a coin, counters in two colours and a dice for the **Game play** activity.

Then encourage discussion of how an addition fact can be used to help find answers to a range of other additions and subtractions through the **Chat room** activity.

PRACTISE

Pupils can then move on to the **Power up** task to provide practice of these skills. Some children may try answering the questions without using the given fact, but encourage them to see the link between each question and the given fact and ask them to explain their reasoning. The focus should be less on answering the questions and more on understanding how facts relate to each other.

APPLY

The **Explore** activity involves worded problems in real-life contexts. Ensure that children record a number sentence for each and not just the answer.

Unit 2B Partitioning, calculating and checking PB pp 26 & 27

TEACH

Begin by discussing how addition facts and subtraction facts relate to each other, inviting children to suggest related facts for a given addition. Children should then tackle the **Plug in** activity.

Then introduce the two methods of addition outlined in the first **Chat room** activity, i.e. using an empty number line to count on, and using partitioning. Demonstrate these methods carefully, ensuring children understand how both methods reach the answer, encouraging children to come to the front and try the methods themselves for other questions.

PRACTISE

Then pupils can choose questions from the **Power up** exercise to answer using either method (or both). Similarly the second **Chat room** activity can be explored to demonstrate subtraction. Show a third method using a 100 square, where, to subtract 19 you move up 2 columns from the initial number (to subtract 20) and then move on one to adjust. Some children may prefer this more pictorial approach and can be given a 100 square to use themselves. The **Game play** activity provides practice in adding and subtracting 2-digit numbers and requires PCM 3, a counter per player, a dice per pair and coloured pencils.

APPLY

For the **Explore** activity pupils can create their own additions and subtractions using the digits given. Encourage them to work systematically to find as many calculations as they can.

Unit 2C Making decisions about calculations

PB pp 28 & 29

TEACH

Begin by asking some oral questions about pairs of numbers with a total of 100, starting with multiples of 10. Introduce other pairs of 2-digit numbers and encourage pupils to add the two numbers to ensure that the total is 100, and not 110, e.g. 72 and 38, and ask them to complete the **Plug in** activity and check their answers in this way.

The **Power up** exercise provides opportunity for children to make decisions about appropriate number sentences when solving calculation problems. To reinforce this further, ask children to make up questions for the other number sentences in each question.

For missing-number calculations children may need to use the inverse calculation to find the missing number each time. This can be discussed and explored through the **Chat room** activity, together with considering whether calculations can be done mentally or with jottings.

PRACTISE

The **Game play** activity provides opportunity for children to make decisions about problems and to identify suitable number sentences that could be used to solve it. Pupils in each pair will require counters in two colours and the cards from PCM 4. To assess the children's work, they could be asked to copy the missing number sentence they chose onto the back of the card each time. The cards could then be used for further practice work.

APPLY

The **Explore** activity can be used to encourage quick mental subtraction where children make decisions about whether differences can be found without writing anything down. To extend this activity further, if required, children can draw their own similar diagrams.

Unit 2D Choosing and using efficient methods

PB pp 30 & 31

TEACH

Introduce the **Plug in** activity and discuss how the lengths of the lines can be represented as subtraction facts. Then consider the two methods of subtraction outlined in the **Chat room** activity, i.e. using an empty number line to count on from the smaller number up to the larger number and counting back from the larger number to the smaller number to find the difference. Demonstrate these methods carefully, ensuring children understand how both methods reach the answer, encouraging children to come to the front and try the methods themselves for other questions.

PRACTISE

Children can then find differences using these methods in the **Power up** exercise. They should be encouraged to check their solutions using addition. When these subtractions have been tried, discuss the methods used and introduce the question 67 – 9. Discuss whether either of the two methods shown would be appropriate for this question and encourage children to explain why not. Show that it would be more effective to count back 9 from 67 rather than counting on from 9 to 67.

The final **Power up** question provides opportunity for children to use efficient methods to find totals. Allow time for discussion of the methods used to find these totals at the end.

The **Game play** activity can be used if further practice in addition is required. Similarly, the rules can be changed to see which player has the larger difference, rather than total, to reinforce subtraction skills further.

APPLY

Read through the word problems in the **Explore** activity and encourage children to identify suitable number sentences to help solve the problems. It is vital that the answers are checked by re-reading the problem as it is very easy for children to make mistakes in such questions. As a group, go over each question carefully discussing the methods used.

Answers
System scans

Unit 2 (PB p6)
1a 5 **b** 14 **c** 130 **d** 50 **e** 93 **f** 73 **g** 65 **h** 180
2a 8 + 7 = 15, 15 − 7 = 8, 15 − 8 = 7
b 13 − 7 = 6, 6 + 7 = 13, 7 + 6 = 13

3a Number sentence such as
100 − □ = 22 or 100 − 22 = □. Answer = 78 cm
3b Number sentence such as
□ + 85 = 100 or 100 − 85 = □. Answer = 15 people
3c Number sentence such as
□ − 38 = 48 or 38 + 48 = □. Answer = £86

4a 95 **b** 71 **c** 37 **d** 54

Pupil's Book questions

Unit 2A (PB pp 24–25)
Plug in: **a** 10 **b** 4 **c** 13 **d** 11 **e** 4 **f** 14 **g** 11 **h** 8
i 15 **j** 4 **k** 12 **l** 17 **m** 5 **n** 14

Chat room: 7 + 6 = 13   6 + 8 = 14   13 − 7 = 6   60 + 70 = 130   46 + 7 = 53   63 − 7 = 56

Power up: **a** 7 **b** 16 **c** 150 **d** 70 **e** 75 **f** 35 **g** 67 **h** 88

Explore: **1** 74 − 46 = 28   **2** 460 + 280 = 740
3 28 + 46 = 74   **4** 74 − 46 = 28   **5** 740 − 280 = 460
6 46 + 28 = 74

Unit 2B (PB pp 26–27)
Plug in: **a** 8 + 3 = 11, 3 + 8 = 11, 11 − 8 = 3, 11 − 3 = 8
b 16 − 7 = 9, 16 − 9 = 7, 7 + 9 = 16, 9 + 7 = 16
c 25 − 9 = 16, 25 − 16 = 9, 9 + 16 = 25, 16 + 9 = 25

Power up: 28 + 37 = 65   53 + 26 = 79   47 + 34 = 81
26 + 17 = 43   33 + 26 = 59   45 + 27 = 72   18 + 64 = 82
37 + 27 = 64

Unit 2C (PB pp 28–29)
Plug in: **a** C **b** D **c** C **d** B **e** C
Power up: **1** 20 − 8 = 12   **2** 40 − 25 = 15
3 25 − 14 = 11

Unit 2D (PB pp 30–31)
Plug in: 18 − 4 = 14   20 − 9 = 11   14 − 7 = 7
12 − 1 = 11   16 − 7 = 9, 17 − 10 = 7
19 − 3 = 16   20 − 6 = 14   17 − 9 = 8   14 − 5 = 9,
12 − 3 = 9   20 − 3 = 17

Explore: **1** 32 kg + 12 kg = 44 kg   **2** 46 kg − 17 kg = 29 kg
3 18 kg + 27 kg = 45 kg   **4** 65 kg − 29 kg = 36 kg

Check-up scans

2A Using known facts to find others (p58)

1	**a**		**b**	
		16		18
		18		20
		14		18
	17 16 15		15 24 17	

2a 70 **b** 160 **c** 120 **d** 50 **e** 50 **f** 30
3a 17 **b** 75 **c** 550 **d** 170 **e** 3800 **f** 27
Train your brain!
Any related facts such as: 360 + 470 = 83 or 83 − 47 = 38, etc.

2B Partitioning, calculating and checking (p59)
1a 30 + 9 **b** 20 + 8 **c** 70 + 4
2a 79 **b** 81 **c** 91
3a 58 + 36 = 94   **b** 94 − 36 = 58 or 94 − 58 = 34
4   83
Train your brain! Possible answers:
45 + 78 or 48 + 75 = 123,   47 + 58 or 48 + 57 = 105,
54 + 78 or 58 + 74 = 132,
54 + 87 or 57 + 84 = 141,   74 + 85 or 75 + 84 = 159,
45 + 87 or 47 + 85 = 132

2C Making decisions about calculations (p60)
1a 20 − 11 = 9   **b** 21 − 12 = 9
2a 53 **b** 82 **c** 33 **d** 53 **e** 15 **f** 85
3 £47: Either 47 + 38 = 85 or 85 − 38 = 47

2D Choosing and using effective methods (p61)
1 63 − 45 = 18 or 63 − 18 = 45
2 93 − 48 = 45
3a 54 **b** 28 **c** 58
Train your brain! Possible answers:
78 − 45 = 33, 75 − 48 = 27,   58 − 47 = 11,   57 − 48 = 9,
78 − 54 = 24,   74 − 58 = 16,
87 − 54 = 33, 84 − 57 = 27,   85 − 74 = 11,   84 − 75 = 9,
87 − 45 = 42,   85 − 47 = 38

Unit 3 Understanding and using multiplication and division

Objectives

PB pages 32–41 Understanding multiplication and divsion

• recognise when situations involving repeated addition are more efficiently represented using multiplication • use known facts to work out related ones, for example, use 3 × 4 = 12 to answer 30 × 4 or 120 ÷ 40	**Lesson 3A** PB pp 32, 33 PCM 5
• recognise when situations involving equal sharing or grouping or repeated subtraction are more efficiently represented using division • use known facts to work out related ones, for example, use 3 × 4 = 12 to answer 30 × 4 or 120 ÷ 40	**Lesson 3B** PB pp 34, 35 PCM 6
• represent arrays using multiplication and carry out multiplication calculations using arrays • use partitioning to multiply a two-digit number by a single-digit number and record steps	**Lesson 3C** PB pp 36, 37
• interpret division as the inverse of multiplication, for example, understanding that 24 ÷ 4 can be found using 4 × 6 = 24 • divide a two-digit by a single-digit number by splitting it into sensible chunks • find and interpret remainders in division, rounding up or down where appropriate	**Lesson 3D** PB pp 38, 39
• find a unit fraction, for example, 1/5 of an amount using division, then multiply the answer to find non-unit fractions, for example, 2/5, 3/5	**Lesson 3E** PB pp 40, 41 PCM 7

Key vocabulary

digit, place value, number, numeral, position, units/ones, tens, hundreds, number lines, multiple, multiply, divide, share, product, times, groups of, lots of, equal groups, counting on, counting back, number sentence, recall, method, chunking, array

Teaching resources, ideas and mental starters

ITP software, squared paper, arrays, cubes, counters, counting equipment, bricks, base 10 materials, bead strings, number lines

Counting sticks and number lines can be used to count on and back in equal steps to and from zero.

Bead strings for dividing 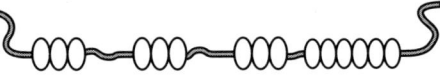 and arrays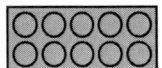

Review and access prior learning

Errors and misconceptions – System scan 3

1   Assist children with the first addition and multiplication, e.g. 3 + 3 + 3 + 3 + 3 and 5 × 3. Then note whether they can apply these ideas to find another multiplication and do the same for the next set. Observe whether the child resorts to counting spots to find the answers or whether counting on or tables facts are used.

2   Provide counting equipment if necessary. Encourage children to explain how they worked out each answer. Observe whether they share out objects, use known tables facts or whether they use some other method.

3   Does the child understand multiplication as an array? Can they use this idea more abstractly to work out the answer to 4 × 26? Provide further questions of this type to assess this in more detail if necessary.

4   Observe whether the child uses a chunking method or a different approach. Do they understand remainders and record them appropriately?

5, 6   Is the child able to find a unit fraction (numerator 1) of a number? Is division used? Observe whether practical materials are needed or whether knowledge of tables facts is secure and drawn upon

Unit 3A Understanding multiplication

PB pp 32 & 33

PCM 5

TEACH

Work together to complete the **Plug in** activity, revising counting on in equal steps from zero. Note which multiples children are most familiar with and use a counting stick to practise those more difficult multiples to remember.

Remind children of the link between repeated addition and multiplication by looking together at the **Power up** exercise. Use appropriate vocabulary to describe the multiplications, e.g. 4 times 3 or 4 multiplied by 3, or 4 lots of 3, or 4 groups of 3, etc. and encourage children to read the facts aloud. Ensure that children understand the × sign and what it represents. Encourage children to notice that 4 × 5 can represent 4 lots of 5 spots or 4 spots multiplied by 5. Stress that 4 × 5 and 5 × 4 produce the same answer.

PRACTISE

The **Game play** activity helps children to become more confident with understanding the link between repeated addition and multiplication sentences. Provide pupils in each pair with a copy of the cards on PCM 5. Encourage children, in pairs, to discuss the **Chat room** activity and identify how 5 × 7 could be 5 lots of 7 spots or 7 lots of 5 spots.

APPLY

Read through the word problems in the **Explore** activity. Some children may try answering the questions without using the given fact, but encourage them to see the link between each question and the given fact and ask them to explain their reasoning. The focus should be less on answering the questions and more on understanding how facts relate to each other. Some pupils may require support in appreciating the link between multiplication and division facts.

Unit 3B Understanding division

PB pp 34 & 35

PCM 6

TEACH

Begin by counting back in steps of 2 from 20, steps of 5 from 50 and steps of 10 from 100 before asking children to complete the **Plug in** activity. Then allow children time in pairs to look at the **Chat room** activity and encourage pupils to notice the difference between sorting into groups of 7 or sorting into 7 groups. Explain that both can be described as dividing by 7.

PRACTISE

Provide pupils with cubes for the **Power up** exercise and encourage them to sort into groups of the given size and also to sort into that many groups and notice that the answers are the same. Draw attention to which way each child has chosen to work.

The **Game play** activity requires the cards from PCM 6. Children arrange the cards to make true statements and should be encouraged to record each as a division statement using numbers and the division sign.

APPLY

Read through the word problems in the **Explore** activity. Some children may try answering the questions without using the given fact, but encourage them to see the link between each question and the given fact and ask them to explain their reasoning. The focus should be less on answering the questions and more on understanding how facts relate to each other. Some pupils may require support in appreciating the link between multiplication and division facts.

Unit 3C Using multiplication strategies   PB pp 36 & 37

TEACH

The **Plug in** activity provides times tables practice and children should be encouraged to work quickly. Remind children that any number multiplied by zero gives the answer zero, and encourage children to consider this idea in real circumstances, e.g. *I am given no lots of sweets.*

Introduce the idea of arrays to represent multiplication facts through the first **Power up** exercise. Look at the example together and encourage children to write pairs of multiplication facts for each brick.

PRACTISE

Encourage children, in pairs, to use dice to create multiplication questions and to show them as arrays on squared paper, as part of the **Game play** activity. The **Chat room** activity can help pupils to begin to see how arrays can help them to answer more difficult multiplication questions, e.g. to answer 4 × 13 by multiplying 4 by 10 and 4 by 3 and adding the parts together. Invite children to discuss the examples in pairs and to work out other similar multiplications in this way. The second **Power up** exercise involves matching arrays with given questions. Children should then use these to find the answers.

APPLY

The **Explore** section involves real-life problems requiring multiplication. Further questions of this type can be given to children to reinforce these ideas further.

Unit 3D Using division strategies   PB pp 38 & 39

TEACH

Look at the example in the **Plug in** activity and discuss how the numbers in each triangle can be used to create two multiplication and two division facts. Invite children to write sets of four facts for some or all of the triangles shown.

Look at the information boxes in the **Chat room** activity. Demonstrate the method carefully, ensuring children understand how it works, and encourage children to come to the front and try the method themselves for other similar questions. Ensure that children understand how to work out the answer in this method and how to show remainders.

The method could also be shown on a number line, if preferred, e.g. for 42 ÷ 3 the following line could be drawn.

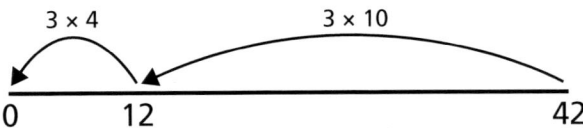

PRACTISE

Children can then tackle the division questions in the **Power up** exercise, using a similar strategy. They should then write related facts for each. The optional **Game play** activity provides further reinforcement of division of a two-digit number by a single digit. Pupils need three dice per pair for the game.

APPLY

When introducing the **Explore** activity it is vital to explain to children that sometimes in situations in real life, where a division has an answer with a remainder, it is necessary to round the answer up or down. Go through the questions shown and discuss the first few, asking children to explain why they must round the answer up or down in each case.

Unit 3E Finding fractions

PB pp 40 & 41

TEACH

Revise the idea that finding one third is the same as dividing by 3 and ask children to tackle the **Plug in** activity, recalling answers as quickly as they can. Draw attention to the fact that any unit fraction (i.e. any fraction with the numerator 1) of a number can be found by dividing the number by the denominator (the bottom number). To practise this idea, ask pupils to try the first **Power up** exercise and to use division to work out the answers.

Then allow opportunity for children to discuss the statements in the **Chat room** activity and to say which they think are true and which are false. Through consideration of this ensure that children appreciate that when finding any fraction of a number they can divide to find the unit fraction first and then multiply to find another fraction, e.g. $\frac{3}{5}$ of 20 is found by finding $\frac{1}{5}$ of 20 (4) and then multiplying the answer by 3. Show this pictorially if necessary, by showing $\frac{3}{5}$ of a shape and writing 4 inside each fifth.

PRACTISE

Ask children to practice finding fractions of amounts through the second **Power up** exercise and discuss the answers together at the end. For further reinforcement, and if there is time, provide the game cards from PCM 7 and ask children to try the **Game play** activity in pairs.

APPLY

The **Explore** activity gives further opportunity for children to find fractions of amounts with larger numbers. Children could also make up more questions of their own like these.

Answers
System scans
Unit 3 (PB p7)
1a 3 + 3 + 3 + 3 + 3 = 15, 5 × 3 = 15,
3 × 5 = 15 **b** 4 + 4 + 4 + 4 + 4 + 4 = 24,
4 × 6 = 24, 6 × 4 = 24
2a 4 **b** 10 **c** 6 **d** 8 **e** 4 **f** 7
3a 4 × 5 = 20, 5 × 4 = 20 **b** 3 × 6 = 18, 6 × 3 = 18
c 4 × 6 = 24, 6 × 4 = 24
4 104
5a 16 r 3 **b** 16 r 3 **c** 17 r 1
6a £3 **b** £4 **c** £50 **d** £10 **e** £21 **f** £24

Pupil's Book questions
Unit 3A (PB pp 32–33)
Plug in:
1 0, 5, 10, 15, 20, 25, 30, 35, 40, 45, 50
2 0, 3, 6, 9, 12, 15, 18, 21, 24, 26, 30
3 0, 4, 8, 12, 16, 20, 24, 28, 32, 36, 40
4 0, 6, 12, 18, 24, 30, 36, 42, 48, 54, 60

Power up:
1a 2 + 2 + 2 + 2 + 2 = 10, 5 × 2 = 10, 2 × 5 = 10
b 3 + 3 + 3 + 3 + 3 + 3 = 18, 6 × 3 = 18, 3 × 6 = 18
c 6 + 6 + 6 + 6 = 24, 4 × 6 = 24, 6 × 4 = 24
d 8 + 8 + 8 = 24, 3 × 8 = 24, 8 × 3 = 24
e 5 + 5 + 5 + 5 = 20, 4 × 5 = 20, 5 × 4 = 20
f 4 + 4 + 4 + 4 + 4 = 20, 5 × 4 = 20, 4 × 5 = 20
2 The total number of spots is the same:
4 × 5 = 5 × 4 = 20

Explore: 1 4 × 6 = 24 **2** 4 × 60 = 240
3 6 × 40p = 240p (or £2.40) **4** 24 ÷ 6 = 4
5 6 × 40 = 240

Unit 3B (PB pp 34–35)
Plug in: 1 21, 18, 15, 12, 9, 6, 3
2 28, 24, 20, 16, 12, 8, 4 **3** 42, 36, 30, 24, 18, 12, 6
Power up: 24 ÷ 4 = 6, 24 ÷ 2 = 12, 24 ÷ 8 = 3,
24 ÷ 3 = 8, 24 ÷ 6 = 4, 24 ÷ 12 = 2
Explore: 1 28 ÷ 7 = 4 **2** £280 ÷ 4 = £70
3 £280 ÷ 7 = £40 **4** 28 ÷ 4 = 7 **5** 280 ÷ 40 = 7
6 £4 × 7 = £28

Unit 3C (PB pp 36–37)
Plug in: a 20 **b** 8 **c** 9 **d** 14 **e** 16 **f** 15 **g** 12
h 8 **i** 24 **j** 0 **k** 70 **l** 25 **m** 45 **n** 12

Power up (1): 1 1 × 3 = 3, 3 × 1 = 3 **2** 2 × 3 = 6,
3 × 2 = 6 **3** 2 × 5 = 10, 5 × 2 = 10 **4** 2 × 6 = 12,
6 × 2 = 12 **5** 2 × 1 = 2, 1 × 2 = 2 **6** 3 × 4 = 12,
4 × 3 = 12 **7** 6 × 1 = 6, 1 × 6 = 6 **8** 3 × 5 = 15,
5 × 3 = 15

Power up (2): a 3 × 18 = 54 **b** 4 × 23 = 92
c 3 × 26 = 78 **d** 7 × 15 = 105 **e** 5 × 17 = 85
Explore: 1 108p or £1.08 **2** 84 sweets **3** 245 minutes

Unit 3D (PB pp 38–39)
Power up: a 18 r 3 **b** 23 **c** 21 r 3 **d** 24 **e** 27 r 1
f 32 r 2

Explore: a 14 **b** 15 **c** 29 **d** 9 **e** 24 **f** 16 **g** 19
h 8 **i** 32 **j** 17 **k** 14 **l** 9

Unit 3E (PB pp 40–41)
Plug in: a 4 **b** 3 **c** 5 **d** 9 **e** 10 **f** 2 **g** 7 **h** 6 **i** 1
j 8
Power up (1): a 16p **b** 9p **c** 10p **d** 9p **e** 10p
f 8p **g** 5p **h** 12p **i** 3p **j** 20p
Chat room: 1 true **2** true **3** false **4** true **5** false
Power up (2): a 24p **b** 36p **c** 50p **d** 18p **e** 70p
f 12p **g** 20p **h** 36p **i** 6p **j** 100p or £1.00
Explore: a 20 **b** 10 **c** 36 **d** 100 **e** 2 **f** 18 **g** 50
h 96 **i** 28

Check-up scans
3A Understanding multiplication (p62)
1a 2 + 2 + 2 + 2 + 2 = 10, 2 × 5 = 10, 5 × 2 = 10
b 3 + 3 + 3 + 3 + 3 + 3 = 18, 3 × 6 = 18, 6 × 3 = 18
2a 7 × 4 = 28 **b** 5 × 6 = 30 **c** 7 × 3 = 21
3a 8 × 5 = 40 **b** 40 ÷ 5 = 8 **c** 40p ÷ 8 = 5p
Train your brain!
1 × 24 = 24, 24 × 1 = 24, 2 × 12 = 24, 12 × 2 = 24,
3 × 8 = 24, 8 × 3 = 24, 4 × 6 = 24, 6 × 4 = 24

3B Understanding division (p63)
1a 70, 60, 50, 40, 30, 20, 10 **b** 35, 30, 25, 20, 15, 10, 5
c 21, 18, 15, 12, 9, 6, 3
2a 6 **b** 6 **c** 6 **d** 6
3a 42 ÷ 7 = 6 **b** £420 ÷ 6 = £70 **c** £420 ÷ 7 = £60
d 420 ÷ 60 = 7
Train your brain!
3 × 8 = 24, 8 × 3 = 24, 24 ÷ 3 = 8

3C Using multiplication strategies (p64)
1a 25 **b** 12 **c** 15 **d** 21 **e** 40 **f** 0 **g** 18 **h** 8
2a 4 × 3 = 12, 3 × 4 = 12 **b** 4 × 5 = 20, 5 × 4 = 20
c 6 × 4 = 24, 4 × 6 = 24
3a 90 **b** 92
4 81
Train your brain!
3 × 17 = 51, 17 × 3 = 51, 51 ÷ 17 = 3

3D Using division strategies (p65)
1a 6 × 7 = 42, 7 × 6 = 42, 42 ÷ 6 = 7, 42 ÷ 7 = 6
b 4 × 8 = 32, 8 × 4 = 32, 32 ÷ 4 = 8, 32 ÷ 8 = 4
2a 23 r 1 **b** 23 r 2 **c** 22 r 1
3a 14 **b** 15

3E Finding fractions (p66)
1a 14 ÷ 7 = 2 **b** 45 ÷ 5 = 9 **c** 40 ÷ 8 = 5
d 100 ÷ 10 = 10
2a £2 **b** £6 **c** £10 **d** £14 **e** £35 **f** £21
3a 14 **b** 10 **c** 280
Train your brain!
1 40
2 25

Objectives

PB pages 42–49
Understanding of Shapes

- name, describe and sort 2-D shapes, using a range of properties including number of sides, equal sides and number of right angles
- compare shapes by describing what is the same and what is different about them
- use Venn and Carroll diagrams to sort shapes according to defined criteria

Lesson 4A
PB pp 42, 43
PCM 8

- name, describe and sort 3-D shapes, using number and shape of faces, number of edges and vertices
- compare shapes by describing what is the same and what is different about them
- use Venn and Carroll diagrams to sort shapes according to defined criteria

Lesson 4B
PB pp 44, 45

- use shape vocabulary accurately, including 2-D, side, vertex, polygon, circle, semicircle, diagonal, regular, irregular, 3-D, face, edge, net, prism, cylinder, sphere
- understand that, in regular shapes, all sides are equal and all angles are equal
- use Venn and Carroll diagrams to sort shapes according to defined criteria

Lesson 4C
PB pp 46, 47

- draw on their practical experience of 2-D and 3-D shapes to visualise shapes, and generate and extend patterns

Lesson 4D
PB pp 48, 49

Key vocabulary

2-D shapes, circle, rectangle, quadrilateral, square, triangle, pentagon, hexagon, heptagon, octagon, decagon, 3-D shapes, cone, sphere, cylinder, cube, cuboid, prism, pyramid, sides, edge, face, vertex/vertices (corners), symmetry, right angle, equal, diagonal, regular, rotation, reflection, angles, convex

Teaching resources, ideas and mental starters

ITP software, pinboards and elastic bands, shape tiles, isometric dotted paper, square dotted paper, squared paper, geostrips, solid shapes, construction kits, hoops for Venn diagram work, interlocking cubes

- Hide a shape in a cloth bag to encourage good descriptions of the features of shapes. Pupils can ask up to 20 questions to help them guess the shape.

- Visualisation of folding and cutting shapes can test children's understanding of the properties of shapes and their symmetries. Provide descriptions for children to imagine.

- Mystery shape: Use Venn and Carroll diagrams and suggest which region of the diagram a mystery shape would sit. Encourage children to draw appropriate shapes towards guessing it.

- Note that for Unit 4D pupils will require dotted paper in a square arrangement.

Review and access prior learning

Errors and misconceptions – System scan 4

1   Ensure children understand that they should say true or false for each. Ask them to say the names of the shapes shown and observe whether they recognise the square, in an unusual orientation, as a square. Ask the children to explain what they think a regular shape is and note whether they can describe equal sides and equal angles.
2   Are the children aware of how a Venn diagram can be used to sort shapes? If they are unable to find the incorrect shape, draw a large Venn diagram and ask children to place other 2-D shapes according to the same criteria.
3   Provide children with solid shapes that match those in the pictures. Note whether children recognise a cylinder even when it is not presented as normally seen (like a tin) or whether they do not recognise its properties. Is the child familiar with the term prism? And can they explain what is special about prisms?
4   Are the children aware of how a Venn diagram can be used to sort shapes? If they are unable to find the incorrect shape, draw a large Venn diagram and ask children to place other 3-D shapes according to the same criteria.
5–7 Read the descriptions of the shapes, providing solid shapes for children if necessary. Encourage them to describe the properties of other 2-D and 3-D shapes to gain a more detailed picture of children's shape concepts.
8   Ask children to look at the shapes in the sequence and to describe what they notice. Do they recognise that the shapes are being rotated through a right angle each time? Can they describe this using appropriate vocabulary?

Unit 4A Comparing and describing 2-D shapes   PB pp 42 & 43

TEACH

Encourage children to visualise and name shapes with 3 sides, 4 sides, 5 sides etc. and ask them to complete the **Plug in** activity. Encourage children, in pairs, to discuss the **Chat room** activity and identify similarities and differences between the shapes in each pair. Ask pairs to record their thinking and discuss these together as a group, emphasising correct vocabulary.

Introduce Venn diagrams and provide an example, demonstrating how they can be used to sort shapes according to their properties.

PRACTISE

Children can then sort the shapes on the cards on PCM 8 as part of the **Power up** exercise. Provide each pair with a large sheet of paper to draw a Venn diagram for themselves. Again, encourage children to work in pairs using shape vocabulary appropriately. The **Game play** activity can provide further opportunity for shape discussion.

APPLY

The **Explore** puzzle requires children to draw shapes to match property descriptions. Allow children time to compare their answers and to discuss similarities and differences between them.

Unit 4B Comparing and describing 3-D shapes   PB pp 44 & 45

TEACH

Give children access to a range of 3-D shapes including a cube, cone, sphere, cylinder, cuboids, prisms and pyramids. Ask them to complete the **Plug in** activity, discussing the meanings of words not known by them, e.g. vertex, edge, etc. Encourage children, in pairs, to discuss the **Chat room** activity and identify similarities and differences between the shapes in each pair. Ask pairs to record their thinking and discuss these together as a group, emphasising correct vocabulary.

Remind the children about Venn diagrams and provide an example, demonstrating how they can be used to sort shapes according to their properties.

PRACTISE

Children can then sort the 3-D solid shapes for the **Power up** exercise. Provide each pair with a large sheet of paper to draw a Venn diagram for themselves. Again, encourage children to work in pairs using shape vocabulary appropriately. The **Game play** activity can provide further opportunity for shape discussion. Pupils will require a dice per pair and counters in two colours.

APPLY

The **Explore** puzzle requires children to match descriptions with real-life 3-D objects shown. Further descriptions of shapes in and around the classroom can be given to provide additional reinforcement.

Unit 4C Sorting and using appropriate shape vocabulary   PB pp 46 & 47

TEACH

For the **Plug in** activity, ensure that children understand that they should say whether statements are true or false. Ask them to correct the mistakes by changing the shape name or altering the description of the properties of the given shape name.

Ask children to play the game in the **Game play** section in pairs. Provide children with a counter each and a dice per pair, together with paper, pencils and rulers. After the game, look at some of the shapes the children have drawn and ask others to suggest which description they might have landed on for each shape.

PRACTISE

Encourage children, in pairs, to talk about and name the shapes in the **Chat room** activity. Provide them with solid shapes and ask them to find a shape to match each present. They should then sort them into a Carroll diagram for the **Power up** exercise. Demonstrate how a Carroll diagram should be used and provide them with a large sheet of paper per pair to sort them. Ensure that they are familiar with the term prism.

APPLY

In the **Explore** problem-solving activity pupils are required to match the descriptions with the related present above.

Unit 4D Generating and extending patterns   PB pp 48 & 49

TEACH

Discuss the sequences in the **Plug in** activity and invite children to describe in their own words how the shapes in each sequence have been altered (e.g. by rotation through one right angle each time).

For the **Power up** exercise, provide children with dotted paper, in a square (not isometric) arrangement. Demonstrate how to divide the sheet up into sets of 4 rows of 4 dots.

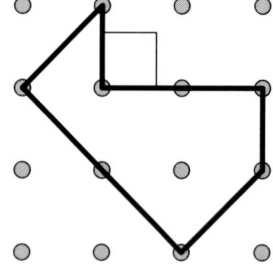

When children are counting the numbers of right angles in each of their hexagons, draw attention to whether the right angle is inside or outside the shape and ensure they only count those inside, e.g. this does not count as a right angle for this shape:

For the **Chat room** activity, ask children to talk to a partner about the pictures of solid shapes made from cubes. Provide them with interlocking cubes, ideally of the colours shown.

PRACTISE

The **Game play** activity helps children to become more familiar with pictures of 3-D shapes made from cubes. Children require cubes, a counter each and a dice per pair. Discuss which shapes are the same but shown from different angles.

APPLY

Using square dotted paper as used in the **Power up** exercise, the **Explore activity** involves drawing shapes to match the descriptions. Further descriptions of shapes can be given to provide further reinforcement.

Answers
System scans
Unit 4 (PB p8)
1a false **b** true **c** true
2 the green triangle   **3a** true **b** true **c** true
4 the pink cylinder   **5** cube   **6** pentagon
7 cylinder   **8** A

Pupil's Book questions
Unit 4A (PB pp 42–43)

Plug in: 1 ☐ , ⬠   **2** pentagon, hexagon, octagon

Game play:
Example routes as shown:

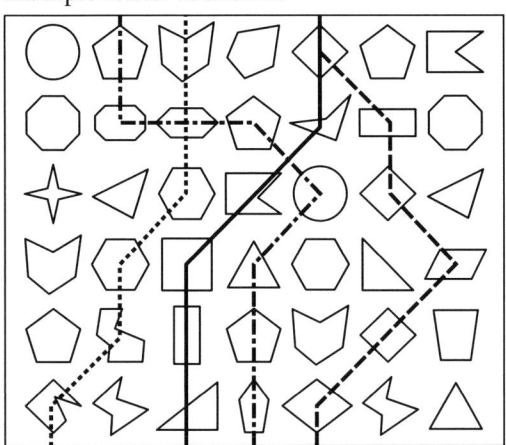

Unit 4B (PB pp 44–45)
Plug in: **1** 6   **2** 1, 1   **3** edges, vertices (corners)   **4** 2, 3
Explore: A the coin/disc   **B** the pack of butter
C the bar of Toblerone

Unit 4C (PB pp 46-47)
Plug in: **1** false   **2** true   **3** false   **4** true   **5** true
Chat room: **A** sphere   **B** cuboid   **C** triangular prism
D hexagonal-based pyramid   **E** cube
F hexagonal prism   **G** cylinder   **H** cone
I square-based pyramid   **J** hemisphere

Power up:

	At least one circular face	No circular faces
A prism	cylinder	cuboid cube triangular prism hexagonal prism
Not a prism	hemisphere cone	sphere pyramids

Explore: **1** F   **2** H   **3** D   **4** J   **5** G   **6** E

Unit 4D (PB pp 48–49)
Plug in: **a** B   **b** A   **c** D

Chat room: **a** 3   **b** 4   **c** 4   **d** 4   **e** 4   **f** 4
b and **f** are the same **c** and **e** might be the same if the hidden cube of shape **e** is purple.

Check-up scans
4A Comparing and describing 2-D shapes (p67)
1 Check six-sided shapes ticked, right angles marked in red, the 2nd shape in row 2 coloured blue.

2

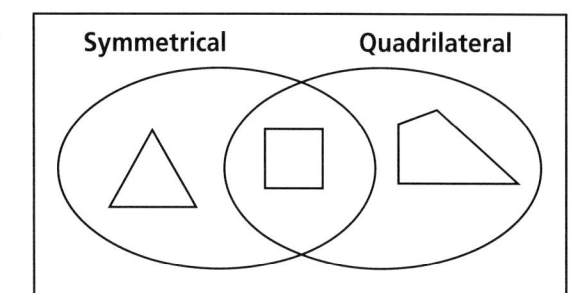

4B Comparing and describing 3-D shapes (p68)
1

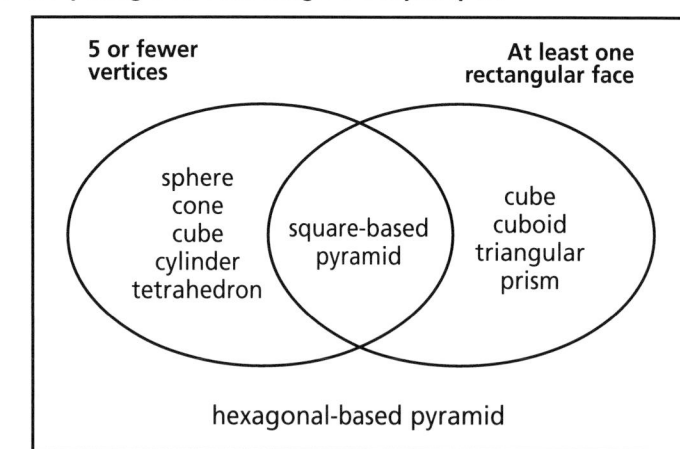

Not all of the shapes in the diagram may have been available.

2a cone   **b** triangular prism

4C Sorting and using appropriate shape vocabulary (p69)
1 Check shapes drawn match the descriptions.

2 Not all of the shapes in the diagram may have been available to pupils.

	At least one triangular face	No triangular faces
A prism	triangular prism	hexagonal prism cylinder
Not a prism	pyramids tetrahedron	sphere cone cube cuboid

4D Generating and extending patterns (p70)
1a A   **b** E
2 Ensure all the shapes have five sides and are different.
3 The 4th shape.

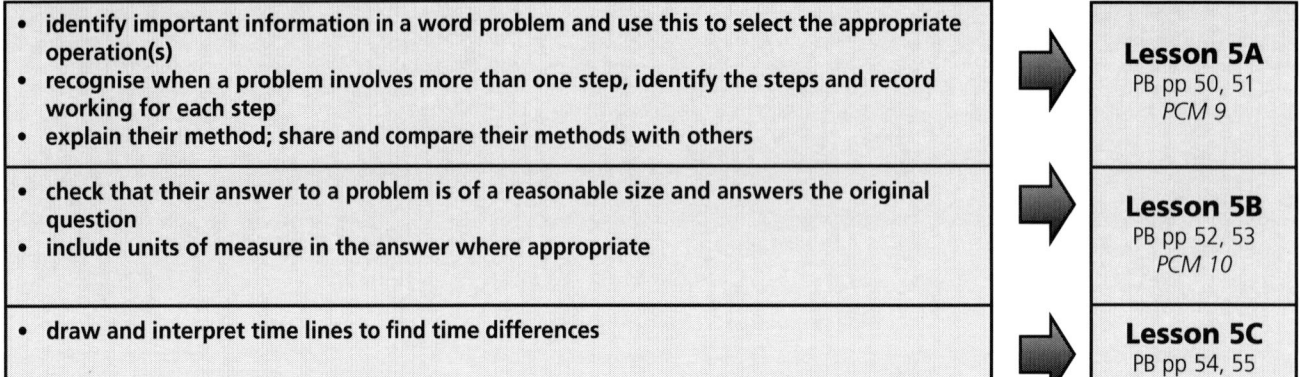

Unit 5 Solving problems involving money and measures

Objectives

PB pages 50–55 Problem solving using money and measures

• identify important information in a word problem and use this to select the appropriate operation(s) • recognise when a problem involves more than one step, identify the steps and record working for each step • explain their method; share and compare their methods with others	**Lesson 5A** PB pp 50, 51 PCM 9
• check that their answer to a problem is of a reasonable size and answers the original question • include units of measure in the answer where appropriate	**Lesson 5B** PB pp 52, 53 PCM 10
• draw and interpret time lines to find time differences	**Lesson 5C** PB pp 54, 55 PCM 11

Key vocabulary

problem, strategy, number, method, calculation, addition, subtraction, multiplication, division, money, pounds, pence, measures, centimetres, metres, kilograms, grams, litres, millilitres, time, clocks, time lines, hours, minutes

Teaching resources, ideas and mental starters

Coins, clocks, measuring equipment, money, price lists, catalogues

Time lines can be used to calculate time differences, e.g. between 3:30 and 6:15:

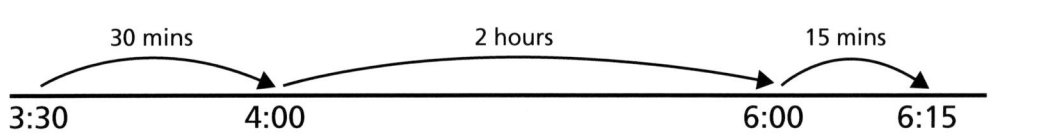
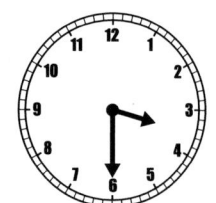

Follow-me/loop cards, such as those on PCMs 9 and 10 can be used in a variety of ways, e.g. they can be given out to a group or an individual or used as a basis for oral questions as a warm up to the lesson.

Review and access prior learning

Errors and misconceptions – System scan 5

1   Read the questions aloud and help children to picture the context. Ask the child to describe what they did and explain the calculations they chose. Does the child use multiplication or addition? Were appropriate strategies used? Were any jottings written down or practical equipment necessary?

2   If the child incorrectly answers the first question, check to see if he/she knows how many grams are the same as one kilogram. If not, provide this information (1000 g = 1 kg) and observe to see if the question, can now be answered. Ask the child to record the number sentence used to find the solution. Can the child verbalise their approach? For the first question, is the child able to correctly subtract 10 g from 500 g?

3   Observe how the child sets about answering these time questions. If unsure, children could be encouraged to use a time line, if they know how. Note whether the child attempts to use some form of subtraction, perhaps incorrectly subtracting 615 from 945.

4   Does the child correctly count back from the times given? Observe the approach used and see whether time lines are drawn.

5   Read the questions through together and note whether the child is able to interpret what the question is asking. What strategies are used? Does the child draw a time line? Does the child experience difficulty with the last two parts, which involve times to the nearest 5 minutes? Provide geared clocks if necessary.

Unit 5A Interpreting and solving word problems   PB pp 50 & 51

TEACH

The **Plug in** activity provides a calculation warm up, revising number facts and requiring quick recall. Introduce the first **Power up** exercise, discussing the context together. Ask children to solve each problem, making decisions about which calculation to use. Remind children of the importance of checking that the final answer given for each problem is a sensible one. Ask children, in pairs, to discuss the **Chat room** activity and to write number sentences to show what they did in question 2. Ensure that they realise that there can be more than one way to record their approach.

PRACTISE

The second **Power up** activity involves an extra step in each calculation. Discuss how each pupil worked the answers out as a whole group, comparing number sentences and strategies used.

The **Game play** loop card activity provides a wider range of problems to solve. The cards from PCM 9 are required. The cards, if arranged in order, should spell out the phrase LOTS OF LOVE.

APPLY

The open-ended **Explore** activity requires children to find different ways that £30 could be spent. Encourage children to work systematically and to find as many solutions as they can.

Unit 5B Checking answers and using units of measure   PB pp 52 & 53

TEACH

The **Plug in** activity revises the relationships between units of measures. Invite children to complete the exercise and then mark their own answers, drawing attention to the correct equivalents where children have made mistakes.

Discuss the information in the **Chat room** section and encourage pupils to see the importance of deciding what to do, estimating, calculating and then checking whether their answer is sensible. Provide some examples to help children understand this, e.g. A *40-year-old grocer has 10 shelves each with 8 tins on. How old is the grocer?* Explain that children have incorrectly given the following answers to this question: 80, 58, even 120! Remind them to think carefully and always give a unit which can help with the checking, e.g. writing 120 years old might have rung some alarm bells!

PRACTISE

Ask pupils to tackle the **Power up** problems using what you have discussed to ensure the answers are sensible. It may be useful to display $1000\,g = 1\,kg$ on the board for children to refer to.

The **Game play** loop card activity provides a wider range of measurement problems to solve. The cards from PCM 10 are required. The cards, if arranged in order, should spell out the word RECTANGLES.

APPLY

The **Explore** activity provide information about some athletics results. Invite children to write their own questions (and answers). These could be read out as a group quiz if there is time.

Unit 5C Using time lines to find time differences

PB pp 54 & 55

TEACH

Begin by showing an analogue clock and as you move the hands around steadily ask children to count on in steps of an equal time size, e.g. each hour, each half hour, etc. Then allow children time to complete the **Plug in** activity, providing geared clocks if any children require further support.

Encourage children, in pairs, to look at the first **Chat room** activity and then discuss the time lines as a whole group. Ask them to explain how the lines are used and provide further questions of this type to demonstrate it fully.

PRACTISE

Encourage children to try the first **Power up** exercise to practise this approach. Provide more questions of this type if any children require more reinforcement. Then examine the second **Chat room** time lines for finding start times of films and invite children to complete the second **Power up** exercise.

Pairs will require a counter and a dice for the **Game play** activity, which provides opportunity for practice of a wider range of time problems. These can be solved using time lines and children could also be provided with geared clocks if necessary.

APPLY

Children will require a copy of the school timetable for the **Explore** activity. Alternative start times for the school day could be given to provide variety, if desired.

Answers

System scans

Unit 5 (PB p9)
1a £29 **b** £38   **2a** 490 g **b** 1900 g or 1.9 kg
3a $3\frac{1}{2}$ hours **b** $2\frac{3}{4}$ hours
4a 5:45 **b** 1:45   **5a** 6:15 **b** 6:20 **c** 6:10

Pupil's Book questions

Unit 5A (PB pp 50–51)
Plug in: **a** 23   **b** 5   **c** 26   **d** 28   **e** 18   **f** 15   **g** 22
h 2

Power up (1): **1a** £10   **b** £12   **c** £26   **d** £14   **e** £24
f £37
2a £10 **b** £5   **c** £6   **3** 6   **4** 20

Power up (2): **1a** £14   **b** £15   **c** £24   **d** £22   **e** £36
f £55

Unit 5B (PB pp 52–53)
Plug in: **a** 100   **b** 1000   **c** 1000   **d** 1000   **e** 4000
f 300   **g** 6000   **h** 8000   **i** 50   **j** 500   **k** 250   **l** 250

Power up: **1** 250 g   **2** 1300 g or 1.3 kg   **3** 500 g
4 900 g   **5** 350 g   **6** 800 g   **7** 2 kg   **8** 1750 g or 1.75 kg

Unit 5C (PB pp 54–55)
Plug in: **a** 10:00, 10:30, 11:00, 11:30, 12:00, 12:30, 1:00
b 4:15, 4:30, 4:45, 5:00, 5:15, 5:30, 5:45
c 5:15, 5:20, 5:25, 5:30, 5:35, 5:40, 5:45, 5:50
d 2:45, 2:50, 2:55, 3:00, 3:05, 3:10, 3:15, 3:20

Power up (1): **1** 1 hour 45 min or $1\frac{3}{4}$ hours
2 1 hour 45 min or $1\frac{3}{4}$ hours
3 2 hours 15 min or $2\frac{1}{4}$ hours

Power up (2): **1** 6:45   **2** 7:30   **3** 7:00

Check-up scans

5A Interpreting and solving word problems (p71)
1 Example answers: **a** $3 \times 8 + 6 = 30$ **b** $4 \times 6 = 24$
c $8 + 3 \times 2 = 14$ **d** $2 \times 6 + 2 \times 2 = 16$
2a 8 years old   **b** 3 tomatoes   **c** 40 people

5B Checking answers and using units of measure (p72)
1a 100   **b** 1000   **c** 1000   **d** 1000
e 4000   **f** 500   **g** 25   **h** 250
2a 600 g   **b** 350 ml   **c** 36 m   **d** 105 cm

5C Using time lines to find time differences (p73)
1a 3:15, 3:20, 3:25, 3:30, 3:35, 3:40
b 7:15, 7:45, 8:15, 8:45, 9:15, 9:45
c 3:45, 3:55, 4:05, 4:15, 4:25, 4:35
2 2 hrs 35 mins
3 2 hrs 25 mins
4a 4:30   **b** 6:20   **c** 5:05

Train your brain!
Check pairs of times are exactly $2\frac{3}{4}$ hrs apart.

Unit 6 Reading and interpreting tables and graphs

Objectives

PB pages 56–63 Problem solving using money and measures

• recognise key features of tables, and diagrams such as frequency charts, pictograms, bar charts, Venn and Carroll diagrams	**Lesson 6A** PB pp 56, 57 *PCM 12*
• use all the information given in a graph or table, including the title and labels, to interpret the data it represents • identify the appropriate column, row or cell of a table to find required information	**Lesson 6B** PB pp 58, 59
• work out the value of each interval on a scale, count along the scale to check and write in unmarked amounts • use their understanding of proportion to make sensible estimates for measures that fall between two marked intervals on a scale	**Lesson 6C** PB pp 60, 61 *PCM 13*
• find and note down all the information needed to solve a problem • identify and carry out the appropriate calculations needed to solve a problem involving data, including questions such as *How many more … ? and How many … altogether?*	**Lesson 6D** PB pp 62, 63

Key vocabulary

graph, chart, table, frequency table, frequency, bar chart, bar-line chart, pictogram, axis, label, scale, cell, column, row, Venn diagram, Carroll diagram, data, estimate, calculation, problem, multiples, tally

Teaching resources, ideas and mental starters

ITP software, squared paper, graphs, tables and charts from magazines and the internet, bus/train/school timetables, data from real-life contexts, calendars, travel brochures, sports results

Counting in equal-sized steps is an important skill underpinning scales on axes. This should be in steps of 2s, 5s, 10s, 25s, 50s, 100s, 200s, 250s, 500s and 1000s for children working at this level.

Counting sticks and number lines can be used to reinforce these ideas further and help children recognise and read scales.

Use unlabelled Venn and Carroll diagrams and write in numbers to encourage children to guess the criteria you are using. Similarly, provide labelled ones and ask children to correctly insert numbers.

Review and access prior learning

Errors and misconceptions – System scan 6

PART A

1 The first question involves a pictogram. Note whether the children notice and understand the key explaining that one picture represents 2 birds. If they do not notice this for themselves, point it out and see if the child chooses to re-examine the answers given. Is the child able to extract the information correctly and make decisions about what calculation to use when necessary? Note whether the child knows what to do to find the total number of birds seen.

2a, b & c Observe whether the child correctly identifies the appropriate cell in the table for each part. Ask further questions about the data in the table to check any errors.

3a & b Does the child appear to understand how a Carroll diagram works? Ask the child to explain why certain numbers are placed in each region. Does the child appear to understand that each cell corresponds to two criteria, one above and one across from the cell?

PART B

1a to e Children often struggle to recognise the value of unmarked numbers on a number line. What strategies does the child use to identify each number? Do they count the intervals or the marks?

2a & b How well does the child read from the conversion chart? Observe whether the child knows to read across and down or up and across from the line to find corresponding equivalents. For the second part, how well is the child able to work out the intermediate points between marked numbers? Provide further questions of this type to assess this in more detail.

3 Ask the child to talk about the bar-line graph and explain what they think it is showing. When they answer the questions, note whether they know to make two readings and then subtract to find the number sold.

Unit 6A Recognising key features of tables and diagrams   PB pp 56 & 57

TEACH

Provide opportunities to count on and back in 2s and 5s, then ask children to complete the **Plug in** activity by continuing the sequences.

Encourage children, in pairs, to discuss the information shown in the **Chat room** section, discussing whether each chart shows the same information and how it is arranged. Invite children to engage with the context by suggesting that each chart has one missing magpie and invite them to explain the effect this would have on each graph. Spend sufficient time discussing the bar chart, frequency table and pictogram, using a range of data vocabulary including the words key, axis, scale, bar, tally, pictogram, etc.

Encourage children to ask their own questions about the charts, such as those beginning with *How many ... ?* or *How many more ... ?*

PRACTISE

The **Power up** exercise provides children with the opportunity to create their own frequency table using tallying and then to draw a bar chart or pictogram of the information. Remind them to label their diagrams correctly and give a title, etc. They will need squared paper for this activity.

Once they have successfully completed their charts, give them a copy of PCM 12 for the **Game play** activity. Here children interpret the information in their chart or pictogram.

APPLY

The **Explore** activity provide children with the opportunity to carry out their own survey, collecting data in a frequency table and then creating their own chart. This could form the basis of a second lesson or could be completed as a homework activity.

Unit 6B Interpreting data in tables and graphs   PB pp 58 & 59

TEACH

The **Plug in** warm-up activity provides children with practice in recalling addition and subtraction facts to 20. Go through the answers and ask children to mark their own work, noting facts they got incorrect and rewriting them correctly. Once completed, ask pairs of children to discuss the information shown in the **Chat room** section, discussing what they think each chart or graph is showing. Ask each pair to say three facts that they have learnt from looking at the charts and to tell them to the rest of the group. Through this, ensure that children have grasped the nature of each graph. Emphasise correct vocabulary including bar chart, bar-line chart, two-way table, axis, scale, bar, row, cell, Venn diagram, etc.

PRACTISE

Ask pupils to answer the questions given in the **Power up** exercise, interpreting the data shown opposite. Remind them to include a unit in the answer if it is needed. Encourage them to note how the same information as shown in the Venn diagram can be placed into a Carroll diagram and help them to appreciate which section corresponds with which one on the Venn diagram.

The **Game play** activity provides practice in gathering information from a table and requires a dice per person.

APPLY

The **Explore** activity can be given as a homework task.

Unit 6C Understanding scales and intervals   PB pp 60 & 61

TEACH

Ask children to count on and back in 10s, 2s, 5s, 20s, 25s, 50s and so on. Children can use the **Plug in** activity
to practise these skills further.

Provide children with PCM 13, a dice and a blue coloured pencil each as part of the **Game play** activity. This quick game can help children to appreciate the value of unnumbered marks on a scale and act as a lead in to the scale work to come.

PRACTISE

Encourage children to work together in pairs to identify the arrowed numbers in the **Chat room** activity. Ask them to explain how they worked out each number, describing their reasoning, for example: *'there are 5 intervals between 0 and 50 so each must be worth 10*, etc. Ensure that they realise that each scale is different from the last. Go through the answers carefully, ensuring that children understand how the size of each interval can be found and that they can use counting on to work out other numbers.

The **Power up** exercise requires children to use what they have been learning about scales in a real graphical context. Ensure children realise that the readings they take will be estimates at times and so answers may be approximate.

APPLY

Discuss the conversion chart shown in **Explore** section and explain how it can be used to find approximate equivalences between inches and centimetres by reading across and down or up and across to the line each time. Ask them to write relationships between the units or provide them with measurements and ask them to find equivalents.

Unit 6D Choosing and carrying out calculations   PB pp 62 & 63

TEACH

For the **Plug in** activity pupils must find the value one half and one quarter of the way along the line. Encourage them to describe how the halfway number can be used to help find the number one quarter of the way along but watch out for children who incorrectly may just halve each number. This strategy only works when the first number on the scale is zero. Further questions about the number three-quarters of the way along could also be asked, if there is time.

Look at the bar-line graph in the **Chat room** section and ask children to talk to a partner about what they think it shows. Ask them to give an explanation of what it shows to the rest of the group. Again, draw attention to the features of the graph, including the scale, the title and the labels on the axes.

PRACTISE

Children can then tackle the questions in the **Power up** exercise, making decisions about what calculations to carry out. Some children may not realise that it is necessary to find the number of cans in the machine at 8am and at 9am and to subtract in order to find the number sold. Encourage them to make their own judgements about the context, including suggesting where this machine might have been sited, etc.

For the **Game play** activity provide children with small blank cards or pieces of paper for them to write questions about the second graph and provide answers too. These can then be read aloud to the group as a quiz.

APPLY

The **Explore** activity involves a real-life situation shown in a table. Children must interpret the information and make decisions about what calculations to use to solve the problems.

Answers
System scans
Unit 6 (PB pp 10–11)
Part A   1a 4   **b** 7   **c** 5   **d** 33   **2a** 14   **b** 11   **c** 3   **3a** 16
b the bottom left section
Part B   1a 100   **b** 300   **c** 400   **d** 600   **e** 750   **2a** about 40 inches   **b** 128 cm (allow any answer between 125 and 130 cm)   **3a** 10   **b** 3pm and 4pm   **c** about 95

Pupil's Book questions
Unit 6A (PB pp 56–57)
Plug in: **a** 25, 30, 35, 40, 45, 50
b 85, 80, 75, 70, 65, 60, 55
c 90, 95, 100, 105, 110, 115, 120

Power up: **1** Frequency table should show the following: green: 6, blue: 9, brown: 10, black: 2, grey: 3

Game play: **1** brown   **2** black   **3** 9   **4** 2   **5** 6   **6** 3
7 1   **8** 3   **9** 30   **10** 21   **11** 27   **12** 12   **13** $\frac{9}{32}$

Unit 6B (PB pp 58–59)
Plug in: **a** 13   **b** 8   **c** 16   **d** 15   **e** 7   **f** 21   **g** 12   **h** 6
i 21   **j** 7   **k** 22   **l** 5   **m** 9   **n** 21
Power up: **1a** 7   **b** 6   **c** 35   **d** 11   **e** 12   **f** 12 m
g 15 m   **h** 6   **i** 1
2

	Multiples of 3	Not multiples of 3
Multiples of 5	15	5, 10, 20
Not multiples of 5	3, 6, 9, 12, 18	1, 2, 4, 7, 8, 11, 13, 14, 16, 17, 19

Unit 6C (PB pp 60–61)
Chat room: **a** 10   **b** 30   **c** 45   **d** 60   **e** 75   **f** 202
g 204   **h** 209   **i** 212   **j** 218
Power up: **1a** 300 cm   **b** 350 cm   **c** 250 cm   **d** 150 cm
e approx 370 cm   **f** approx 330 cm
2a 250 cm   **b** 275 cm   **c** approx 245 cm   **d** 150 cm
e 290 cm   **f** 260 cm

Unit 6D (PB pp 62–63)
Plug in: 1a 50   **b** 150   **c** 30   **d** 250   **e** 100   **f** 750
2a 25   **b** 125   **c** 25   **d** 125   **e** 75   **f** 625
Power up: **1a** 0   **b** 10   **c** 45   **d** 20   **e** 10   **f** 10
2 10am and 11am
3a The machine was filled up.   **b** possibly in a school
c possibly lesson time   **d** 95
Explore: **1** 174   **2** 416   **3** 427

Check-up scans
6A Recognising key features of tables and diagrams (p74)
1a 5   **b** 9   **c** 29
d Check extra $1\frac{1}{2}$ birds drawn in the robin row.
2a Check the sparrow bar drawn to 7.

6B Interpreting data in tables and graphs (p75)
1a 16   **b** 12   **c** 5
2a 27 m   **b** 30 m   **3** 24 m

6C Understanding scales and intervals (p76)
1a 20   **b** 60   **c** 80   **d** 120   **e** 150   **f** 4   **g** 12   **h** 16
i 24   **j** 30   **k** 210   **l** 230   **m** 240   **n** 260   **o** 275
2a 350 cm   **b** about 370 cm

Train your brain!
About 320 cm, about 340 cm

6D Choosing and carrying out calculations (p77)
1a 75   **b** 375   **c** 30   **d** 500
2a 125   **b** 625   **c** 250   **d** 75
3a 10   **b** 12pm to 1pm   **c** 60

900 800 700

600 500 400

300 200 100

[   ] 90 80

70 60 50

40 30 20

10 00 00 9

8 7 6 5 4

3 2 1 0 0

Understanding fractions

Colour the sections of each kaleidoscope to match the fraction descriptions.

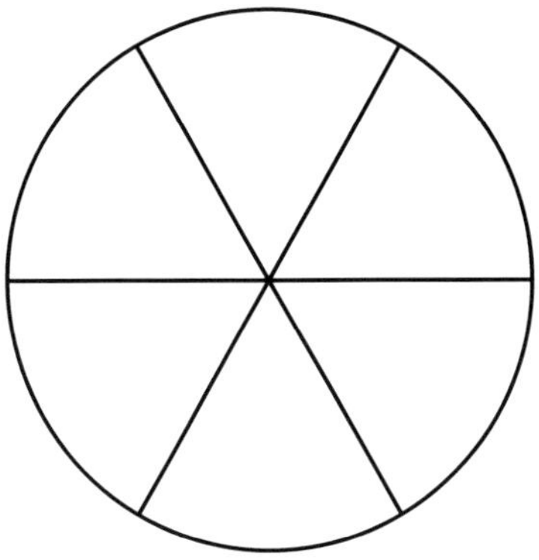

$\frac{1}{6}$ is red

$\frac{2}{6}$ is blue

$\frac{3}{6}$ is yellow

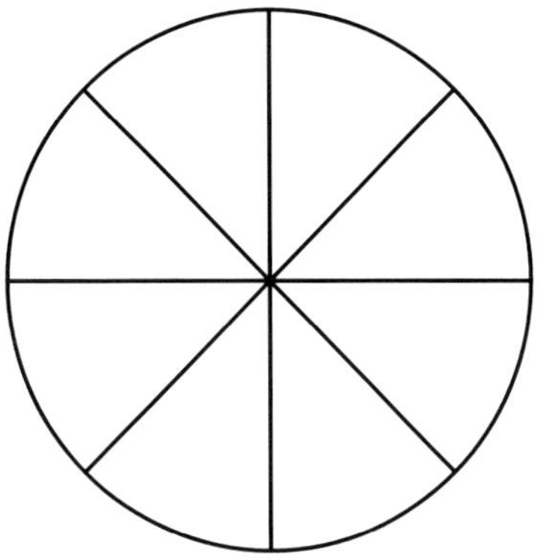

$\frac{1}{8}$ is red

$\frac{3}{8}$ is blue

$\frac{2}{8}$ is yellow

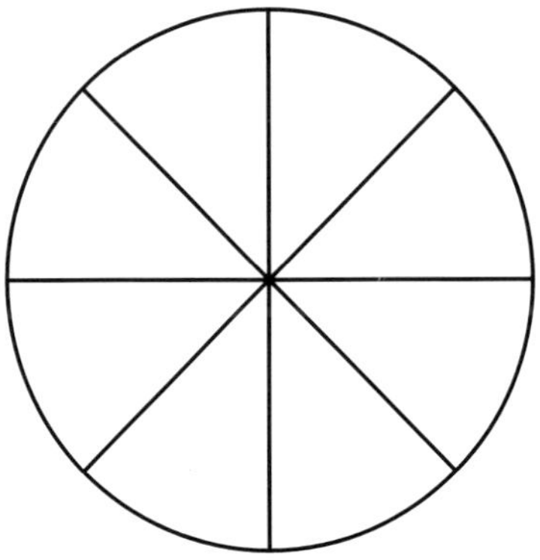

$\frac{4}{8}$ is red

$\frac{1}{8}$ is blue

$\frac{2}{8}$ is yellow

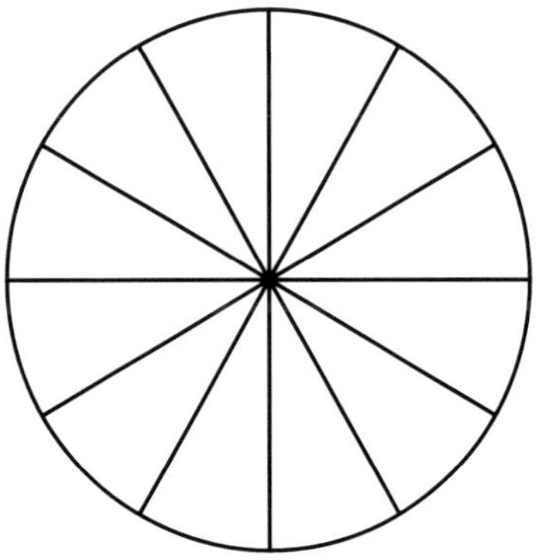

$\frac{3}{12}$ is red

$\frac{5}{12}$ is yellow

$\frac{2}{12}$ is blue

$\frac{1}{12}$ is orange

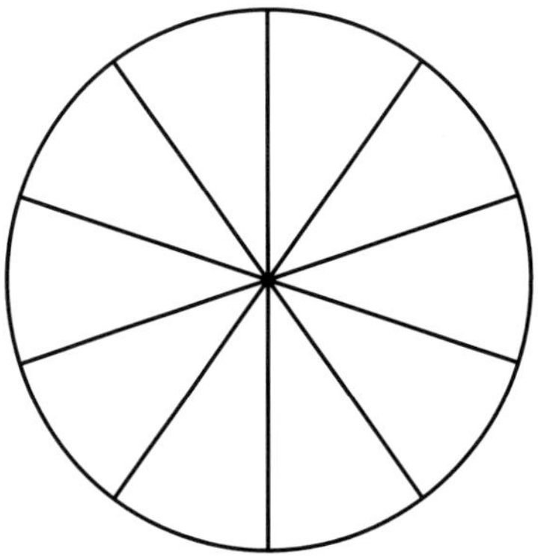

$\frac{2}{10}$ is red

$\frac{1}{10}$ is yellow

$\frac{4}{10}$ is blue

$\frac{3}{10}$ is orange

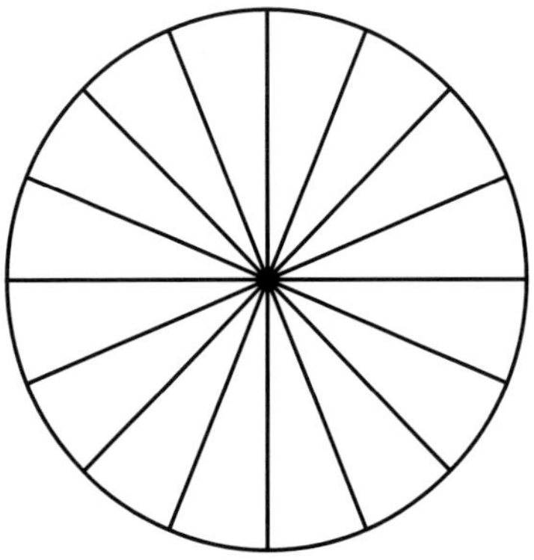

$\frac{1}{16}$ is red

$\frac{7}{16}$ is yellow

$\frac{3}{16}$ is blue

$\frac{4}{16}$ is orange

Cut out the cards to play the game.

© Rising Stars Ltd. 2010

2 players

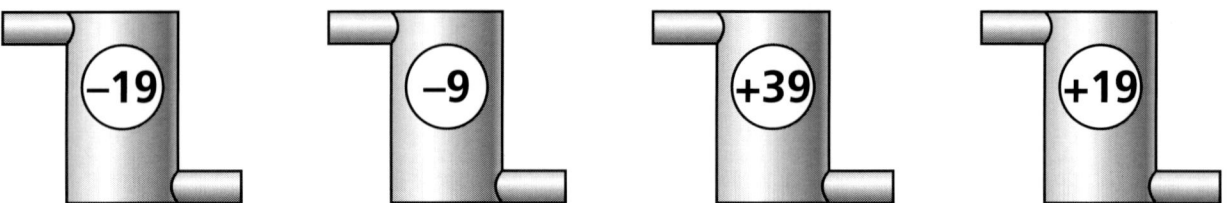

You need a counter each and a dice. Each player chooses a machine.

Take turns to roll the dice and move the counter forward. You must put the number you land on into your machine and work out the answer. Look for the answer further along the line. If you find it, move your counter on to the answer. If not, stay where you are. The winner is the one to reach the finish first.

Start	64	76	55	67	83	103	45	48

								95

103	57	26	36	115	36	84	74

48							

29	65	28	76	20	84	75	55

							59

Finish	85	56	40	123	96	87	68

Making decisions about calculations

There are 47 boys and 85 girls in a school. How many altogether?	I have £85 and I spend £47. How much do I have now?	There are 47 chocolates in a box. 38 of them are milk chocolate. How many are not?
There are 47 cows and some sheep in a field. There are 100 animals altogether. How many are sheep?	I have £85 and I buy a new coat. I have £47 left. How much did I spend?	A farmer collects some eggs. He sells 38 of them and keeps 47 for himself. How many did he collect?
James has some money. He is given £38 more. He now has £85. How much had he at first?	A farmer has 85 pigs and 38 goats. How many animals is this altogether?	A piece of ribbon is 100 cm long. I cut some off. It is now 85 cm long. How much did I cut off?
A book weighs 100 g and an envelope weighs 47 g. Together, what do they weigh?	Paul has 100 g of chocolate. He eats 38 g of it. How much is left?	Mrs Jones is 47. Her father is 38 years older than her. How old is her father?
Kate has 100p. She spends 47p. How much does she have now?	In a jar are some marbles. Jo takes out 47, leaving 85 in the jar. How many were there at the start?	Some people are in a shop. 85 more arrive, making 100 people in total. How many were there at first?
Josh has 47p. He is given some more money. Now he has 100p. How much was he given?	A plank of wood is 100 cm long. Then 85 cm of it is sawn off. How much is left?	Some seeds were planted. 38 of them were eaten by birds. 47 grew. How many seeds were planted?

Understanding multiplication

	3 + 3 + 3 + 3 + 3 + 3 = 18	3 x 6 = 18	6 x 3 = 18
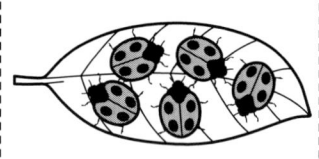	6 + 6 + 6 + 6 = 24	6 x 4 = 24	4 x 6 = 24
	4 + 4 + 4 + 4 + 4 = 20	5 x 4 = 20	4 x 5 = 20
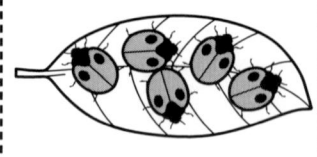	8 + 8 + 8 = 24	3 x 8 = 24	8 x 3 = 24
	2 + 2 + 2 + 2 + 2 = 10	5 x 2 = 10	2 x 5 = 10
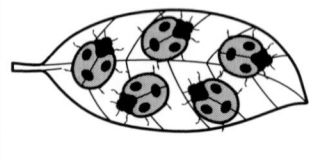	4 + 4 + 4 = 12	3 x 4 = 12	4 x 3 = 12
	3 + 3 + 3 + 3 + 3 = 15	5 x 3 = 15	3 x 5 = 15
	5 + 5 + 5 + 5 + 5 + 5 = 30	6 x 5 = 30	5 x 6 = 30

  © Rising Stars Ltd. 2010

Understanding division

12 oranges	4 people	3 oranges	3 people
9 oranges	6 people	4 oranges	2 people
24 oranges	8 people	6 oranges	1 oranges
18 oranges	9 people	9 oranges	16 oranges

Finding fractions

$\frac{1}{4}$ of 28 gold coins	$\frac{1}{3}$ of 27 gold coins	$\frac{1}{5}$ of 25 gold coins	$\frac{1}{6}$ of 24 gold coins
$\frac{3}{4}$ of 20 gold coins	$\frac{2}{3}$ of 9 gold coins	$\frac{1}{8}$ of 16 gold coins	$\frac{1}{7}$ of 14 gold coins
$\frac{3}{4}$ of 24 gold coins	$\frac{1}{3}$ of 18 gold coins	$\frac{1}{4}$ of 12 gold coins	$\frac{1}{6}$ of 6 gold coins
$\frac{1}{4}$ of 16 gold coins	$\frac{2}{3}$ of 27 gold coins	$\frac{2}{5}$ of 10 gold coins	$\frac{1}{8}$ of 28 gold coins
$\frac{1}{4}$ of 32 gold coins	$\frac{1}{3}$ of 30 gold coins	$\frac{3}{5}$ of 25 gold coins	$\frac{5}{6}$ of 30 gold coins
$\frac{3}{4}$ of 28 gold coins	$\frac{2}{3}$ of 21 gold coins	$\frac{4}{5}$ of 15 gold coins	$\frac{1}{9}$ of 27 gold coins
$\frac{1}{4}$ of 36 gold coins	$\frac{3}{8}$ of 32 gold coins	$\frac{5}{8}$ of 40 gold coins	$\frac{3}{4}$ of 32 gold coins
$\frac{7}{8}$ of 16 gold coins	$\frac{3}{5}$ of 45 gold coins	$\frac{4}{5}$ of 50 gold coins	$\frac{5}{6}$ of 54 gold coins

 © Rising Stars Ltd. 2010

Comparing and describing 2-D shapes

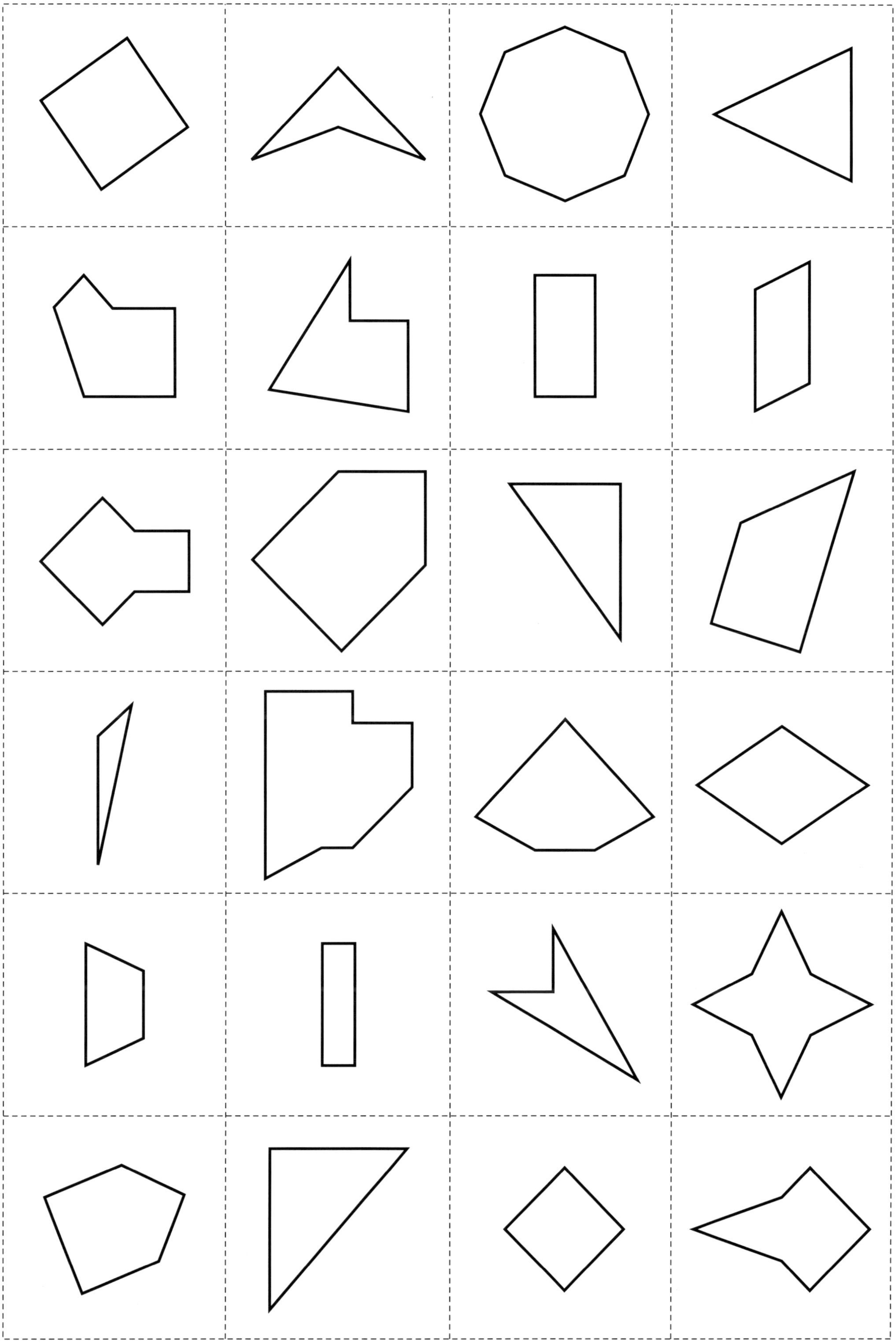

Interpreting and solving word problems

Answer the question on the 'Start' card. Find the answer on one of the other cards.
Then answer that question and so on. Put the cards in a line or loop on the table.

START **7**

A photo album has 5 pages,
with 4 photos on each page.
How many photos altogether?

L

8

Dad is 6 times the age I was last year.
He is 30.
How old am I?

F

40

Al planted 100 seeds. 70 of them
grew into seedlings. He planted half
of these outside.
How many seedlings did he still
have?

O

28

A 24-year-old shopkeeper sells
potatoes in bags of 4. Mrs Jones
needs at least 18 potatoes.
How many bags should she buy?

S

35

Mum had 24 cherry tomatoes. She
ate 6 herself and shared the rest
between her 6 children.
How many did each child get?

V

20

A book has 48 pages. Jo has read half
of the pages.
How many pages has she left to
read?

O

3

A chicken lays 2 eggs each day for
a week.
How many more does the farmer
need to have 21 eggs altogether?

E

5

My sister will be 20 in 4 years' time.
I am half her age.
How old am I?

O

24

A photo album has 6 pages, each
with 4 photos on, and 2 pages with
2 photos on.
How many photos in total?

T

6

There are 12 tents and 4 caravans at
a site. There are 2 people in each
tent and 4 in each caravan. How
many people?

L

 © Rising Stars Ltd. 2010

Checking answers and using units of measure

Answer the question on the 'Start' card. Find the answer on one of the other cards. Then answer that question and so on. Put the cards in a line or loop on the table.

START
25 cm
Jo has a piece of ribbon 12 cm long.
She cuts it in half.
How long is each half?

R

170 cm
Mr Li has 4 lengths of wood, each 2 m long. He puts them end to end in a line. How long is the line?

N

160 cm
A door was 2 m and 10 cm tall.
Jim cut off 5 cm.
How tall is the door now?

L

1 m
A field is half as wide as it is long.
It is 16 m wide.
How long is it?

T

32 m
Sally is 138 cm tall.
Her mum is 32 cm taller.
How tall is her mum?

A

6 cm
A worm grew 4 cm in a week.
Last week it was 9 cm.
How long is it now?

E

17 m
A dog is 50 cm. The dog is twice as tall as a cat.
How tall is the cat?

S

205 cm
A ball of string has 20 m of string.
Dev cuts off 3 m.
How much string is left on the ball?

E

13 cm
A brick is 25 cm long.
What is the length of four bricks in a line?

C

8 m
Sam is 25 cm taller than Pete. Sam is 185 cm tall.
How tall is Pete?

G

Using time lines to find time differences

- Play this game with a friend. You need one counter and a dice.
- Start by placing the counter anywhere on the trail. Take turns to roll the dice and move the counter forward. Answer the question and cross off the time on your time strip. The winner is the first to cross off 5 times in a row.

A TV show starts at 4:30. It lasts for an hour and three-quarters. What time does it end?	Half an hour ago, a TV show started at five minutes to six. What time is it now?	A TV show has been on for an hour and a quarter. The time now is 8:10. What time did it start?
A TV show starts at quarter to five. It lasts for two hours. What time does it end?	(clock showing 12 and pointing to just after 4)	A film lasts for $1\frac{1}{2}$ hours. It will end at twenty past eight. What time did it start?
A film finishes at twenty-five to nine. It has been on for $2\frac{1}{2}$ hours. What time did it start?		A TV show finishes at five past seven. It has been on for 40 minutes. What time did it start?
A quarter of an hour ago, a TV show started at five to six. What time is it now?	(clock showing hands at 11 and 5:30 position)	Three-quarters of an hour ago, a TV show started at 5:35. What time is it now?
A TV show has been on for three-quarters of an hour. It is now 7:20. What time did it start?		A film lasts for $1\frac{1}{4}$ hours. It began at 5:15. What time does it end?
A TV show starts at five to five. It lasts for 1 hour and 45 minutes. What time does it end?	A TV show finishes at half past seven. It has been on for 55 minutes. What time did it start?	A TV show starts at quarter past five. It lasts for 45 minutes. What time does it end?

Player 1's time strip

6:00	6:05	6:10	6:15	6:20	6:25	6:30	6:35	6:40	6:45	6:50	6:55

Player 2's time strip

6:00	6:05	6:10	6:15	6:20	6:25	6:30	6:35	6:40	6:45	6:50	6:55

Recognising key features of tables and diagrams

Follow the trail and answer the questions about the chart you have drawn about eye colours of the children in Class C.

1. Which is the most common eye colour?

_____

2. Which is the least common eye colour?

_____

3. How many children have blue eyes?

_____

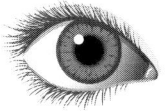 

4. How many children have black eyes?

_____

5. How many children have green eyes?

_____

6. How many more children have green eyes than grey eyes?

_____

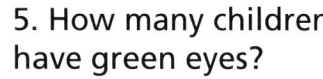

7. How many more children have brown eyes than blue eyes?

_____

 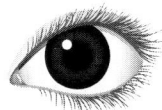

8. How many fewer children have green eyes than blue eyes?

_____

9. How many children are in Class C?

_____

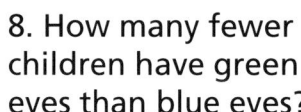

10. How many children in Class C do NOT have blue eyes?

_____

11. How many children in Class C do NOT have grey eyes?

_____

12. Two more children join Class C. Both children have brown eyes. How many children have brown eyes now?

_____

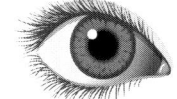 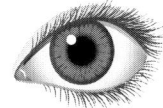

13. What fraction of the class (including the 2 new children) have blue eyes?

_____

You've finished!

© Rising Stars Ltd. 2010

Understanding scales and intervals

Play this game with a partner. You will need a dice.

Take turns to roll the dice. Use the key to find how much water must be added to your container. Use a blue pencil to show each new amount of water. The winner is the first to exactly fill their container.
Miss a go if you roll an amount that is more than you need.

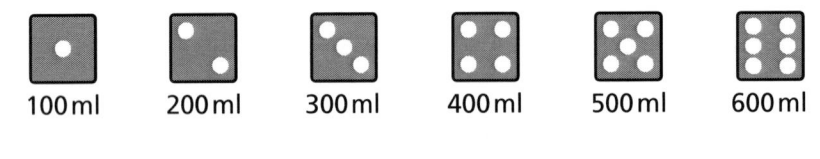

100 ml   200 ml   300 ml   400 ml   500 ml   600 ml

Player 1

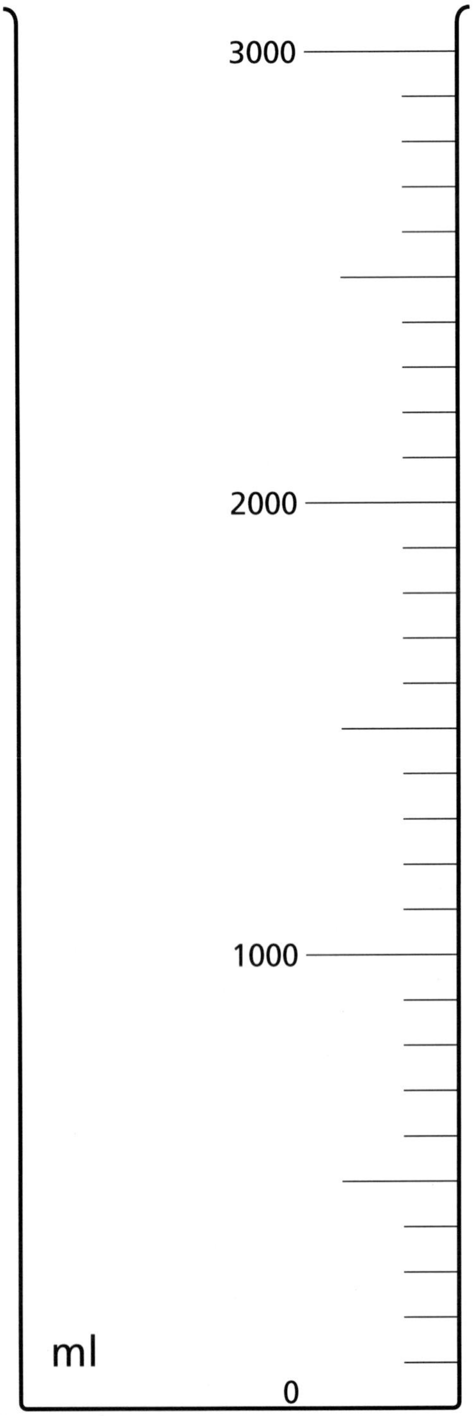

3000

2000

1000

ml

0

Player 2

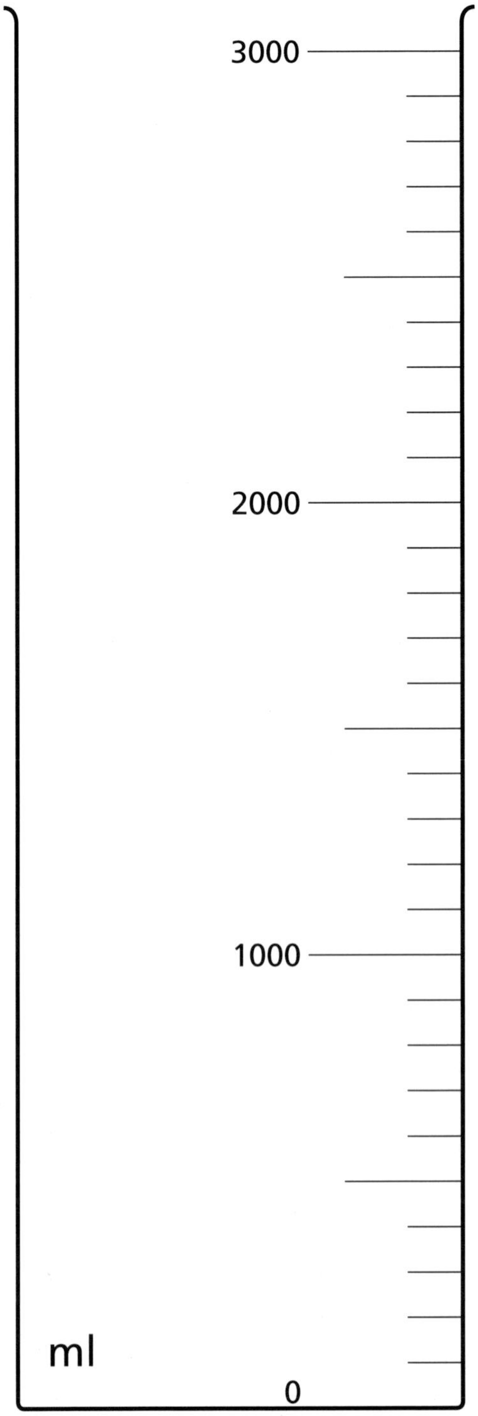

3000

2000

1000

ml

0

Game play (PB page 15)

2 players

You will need a counter each and a dice.

- Take turns to roll the dice and move your counter forward and answer the question.
- If both players land on a question with the same answer you must both go back to the start.

200 × 10	880 ÷ 10	2 × 10	Finish

20 ÷ 10

8 × 10	800 ÷ 10	20 × 10

500 ÷ 10

5 × 10	50 ÷ 10	46 × 10

12 × 10

600 ÷ 10	21 × 10	120 ÷ 10

6 × 10

Start	460 ÷ 10

© Rising Stars Ltd. 2010

Game play (PB page 21)

1 player

You will need: coloured cubes/counters in red, blue, green, yellow and white (at least four in each colour).

Place coloured cubes/counters onto the squares below the line to match those above with the same value.

red	blue	green	yellow	white
two-tenths of a pound	30p	twenty-three 10p coins	2.3m	30cm

230cm

£0.20

20p

three 10p coins

three strips of 10cm

three-tenths of a pound

twenty-three strips of 10cm

three-tenths of a metre

0.3m

£0.30

230p

two 10p coins

£2.30

Game play (PB page 24)

2 players

You will need: a coin, 8 counters (4 of one colour and 4 of another) and a dice.
- Take turns to roll the dice and move the coin around the trail.
- Answer the question you land on and find the answer in the centre.
- If you find it, cover it with one of your coloured counters if you can.
- The winner is the first to have four counters in a line.

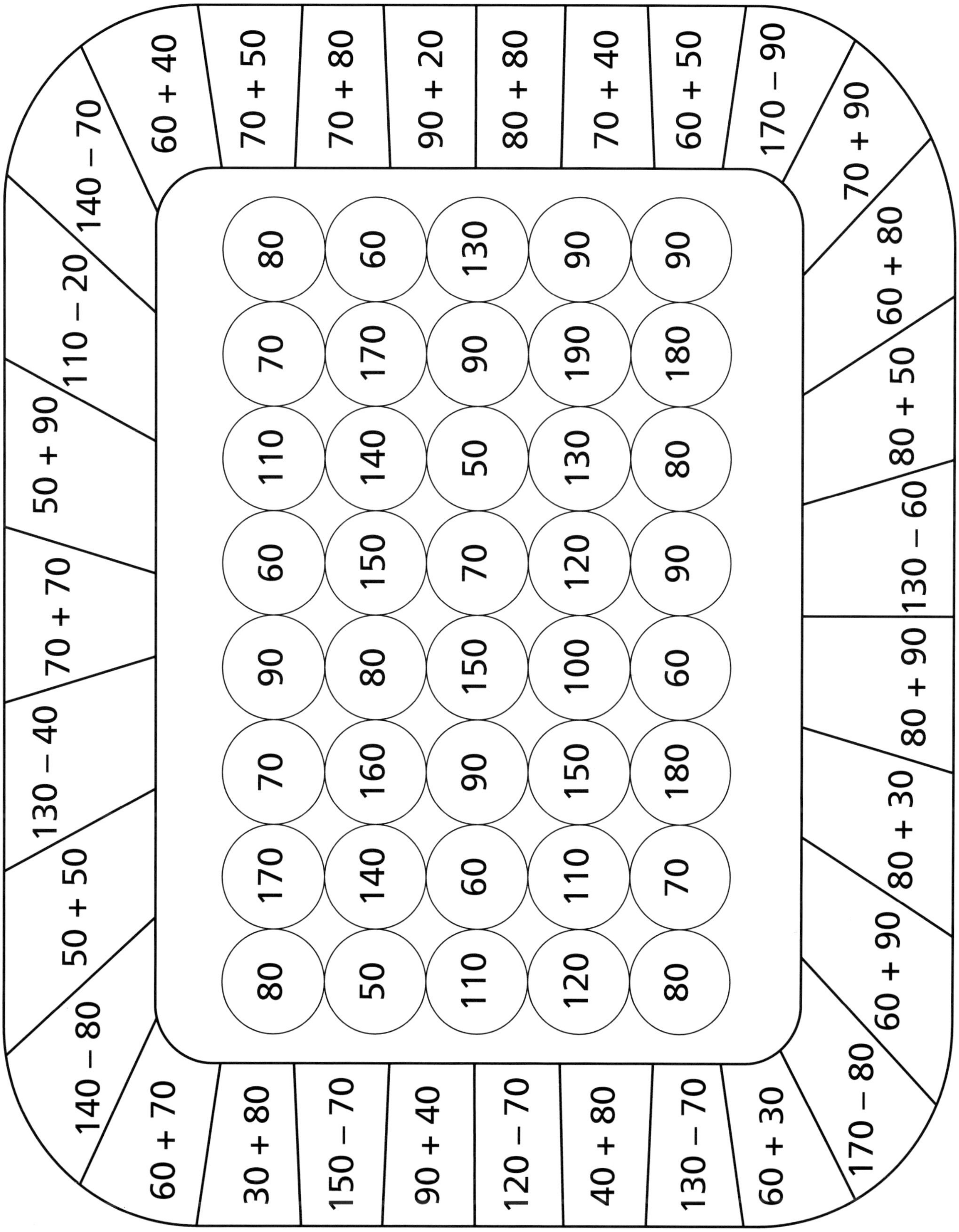

Outer trail (clockwise from top): 60 + 40, 70 + 50, 70 + 80, 90 + 20, 80 + 80, 70 + 40, 60 + 50, 170 − 90, 70 + 90, 60 + 80, 80 + 50, 130 − 60, 80 + 90, 80 + 30, 60 + 90, 170 − 80, 60 + 30, 130 − 70, 40 + 80, 120 − 70, 90 + 40, 150 − 70, 30 + 80, 60 + 70, 140 − 80, 50 + 50, 130 − 40, 70 + 70, 50 + 90, 110 − 20, 140 − 70

Centre grid:

80	60	130	90	90
70	170	90	190	180
110	140	50	130	80
60	150	70	120	90
90	80	150	100	60
70	160	90	150	180
170	140	60	110	70
80	50	110	120	80

Game play (PB page 43)

2 players

You will need: a counter each.

- Each player chooses one of these rules:
  - Jump only on shapes that have more than 5 sides.
  - Jump only on shapes which have at least 1 right angle.
  - Jump only on symmetrical shapes.
  - Jump only on quadrilaterals.

- Place your counter at the bottom side of the square below.

- Take turns to make a move according to your rule. You can move one place each time (vertically, horizontally or diagonally).

- The first player to reach the top side is the winner.

Game play (PB page 45)

2 players

You will need: counters in two colours and a dice.

● Roll the dice and read the related clue. Place a counter in your colour on a shape that matches the clue.

● The winner is the player with counters on the most shapes at the end of the game.

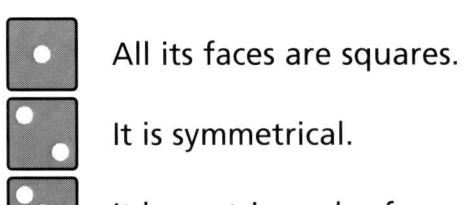

All its faces are squares.

It is symmetrical.

It has a triangular face.

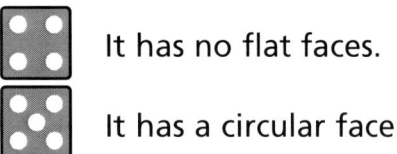

It has no flat faces.

It has a circular face.

It has only rectangular faces.

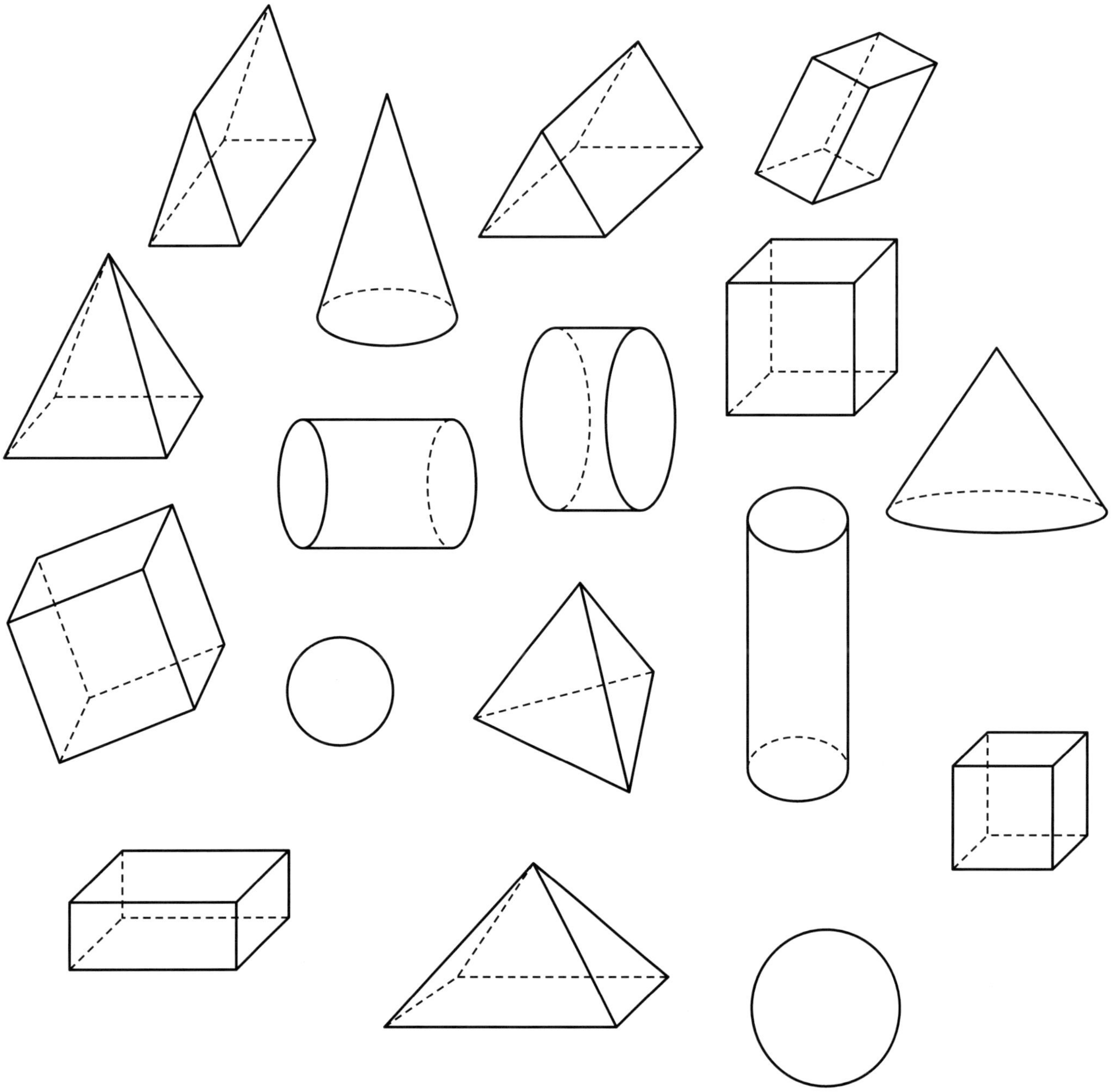

© Rising Stars Ltd. 2010

Game play (PB page 46)

2 players

You will need: a counter each and a dice.

- Roll the dice and draw and name the shape you land on.
- If you do it correctly, stay where you are. If not, move back 4 spaces.
  The winner is the first to reach the finish.

START	a shape with five sides	a shape with four straight sides	a shape with three sides and one right angle	a shape with three right angles
a shape that has one curved side	a shape with ten straight sides	a shape that is regular		a shape that is half a circle
a shape with four lines of symmetry		a shape that is not regular		a symmetrical shape
a shape with four sides but none are equal	**FINISH** a scalene triangle	an equilateral triangle		a shape with no right angles
a regular quadrilateral	a shape with one right angle	a symmetrical shape with six sides		a shape with two right angles and four sides
a shape with six straight sides	a shape with more than four sides	a semicircle		a shape with five straight sides
a shape that is not symmetrical	a shape with eight straight sides	a shape with two lines of symmetry		a shape with one line of symmetry

© Rising Stars Ltd. 2010

Shine!/Level 3   Game play PB p46

Game play (PB page 49)

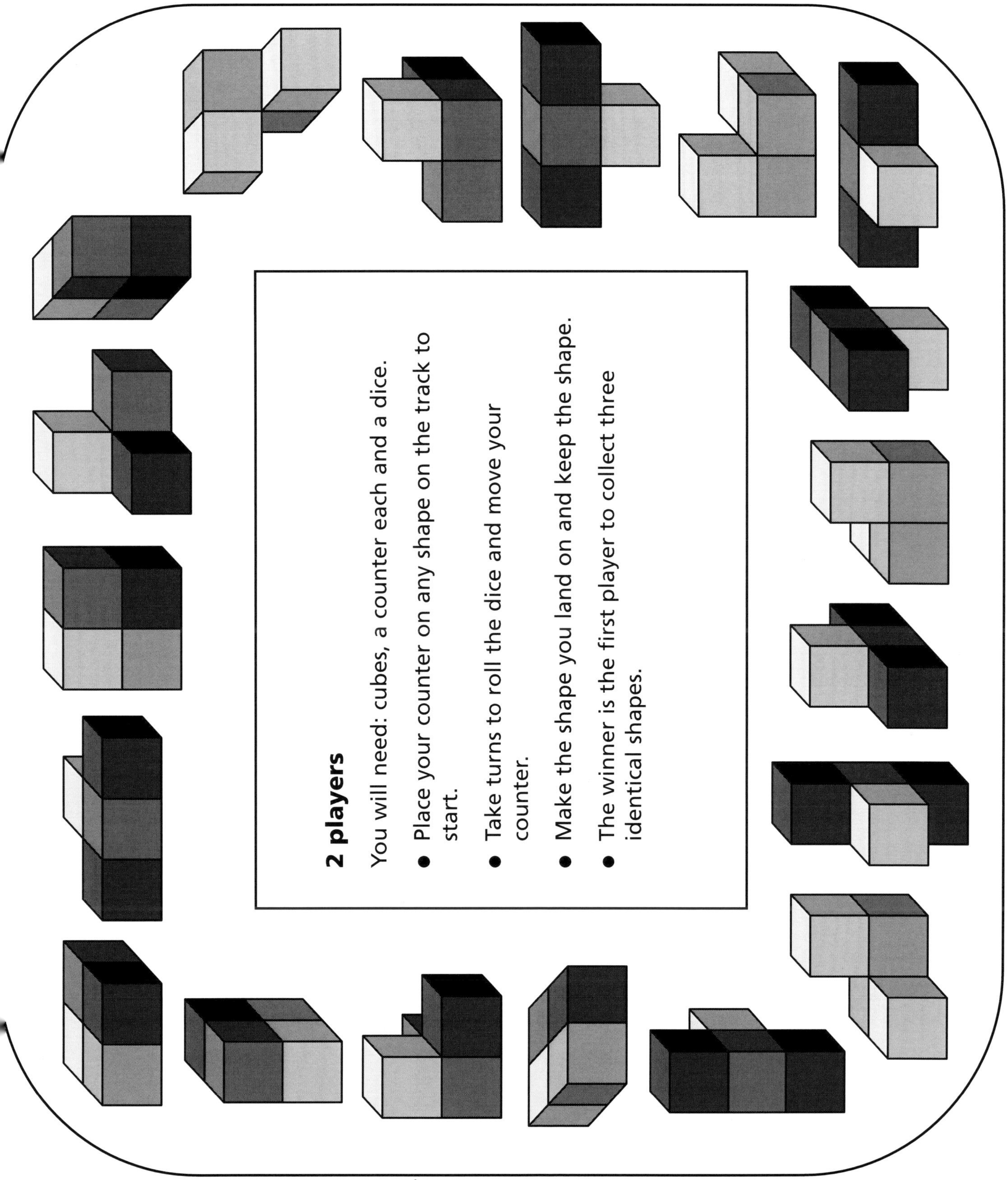

© Rising Stars Ltd. 2010

2 players

You will need: cubes, a counter each and a dice.

- Place your counter on any shape on the track to start.

- Take turns to roll the dice and move your counter.

- Make the shape you land on and keep the shape.

- The winner is the first player to collect three identical shapes.

Check-up scan 1A

1 Write each of these amounts in words.

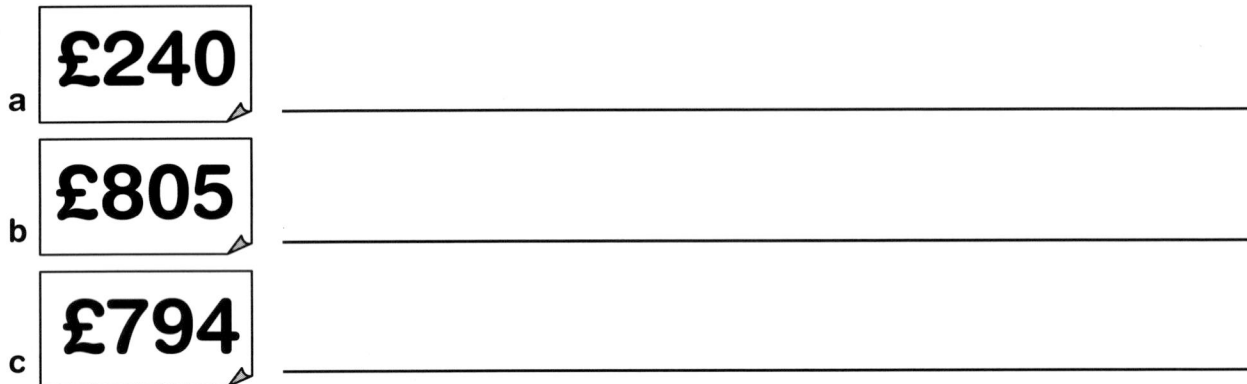

a £240 _____

b £805 _____

c £794 _____

2 Fill in the missing numbers.

a 485 = 400 + _____ + 5   **b** 927 = _____ + 20 + 7

c 382 = _____ + 80 + ___   **d** 609 = _____ + 9

e 573 = _____ + _____ + _____   **f** 310 = ____ + _____ + _____

3 Write these numbers in order, starting with the smallest, to form a sequence.

a 485, 475, 495, 505, 455, 465 _____

b 307, 7, 107, 507, 207, 407 _____

Train your brain!

Write all the possible numbers that can be made using these three digits.
You can use 1, 2 or all 3 of the cards to make a number.
Now write your numbers in order, starting with the smallest.

Then partition each 3-digit number like this: 870 = 800 + 70 + 0

I understand the value of each digit in a three-digit number and can explain how I know. ☐

 © Rising Stars Ltd. 2010   Shine!/Level 3   Check-up scan 1A

Check-up scan 1B

Name: _____

1 Jane says the answer to 48 × 10 is 408. Is she right?

Explain your answer.

2 This machine multiplies numbers by 10. Write in the answer each time.

a  **b**  **c**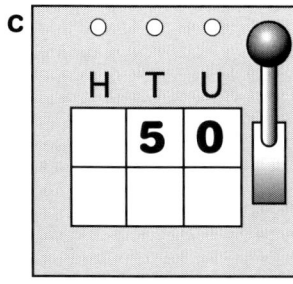

3 10 children sit on each bench. How many children can sit on:

a 7 benches? _____ **b** 12 benches? _____ **c** 60 benches? _____

4 This machine divides numbers by 10. Write in the answer each time.

a 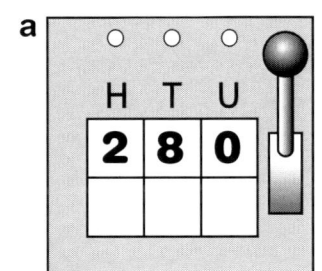 **b**  **c**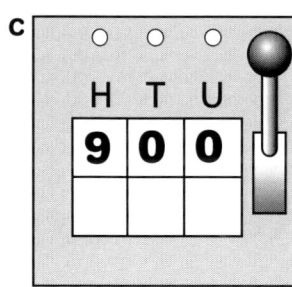

Train your brain!

| 240 | 30 | 300 | 24 | 3 | ×10 = | ÷ 10 = |

Arrange these cards to make as many different true statements as you can.

I can multiply/divide a number by 10.

© Rising Stars Ltd. 2010

Check-up scan 1C

Name: _____

1   Round each of these numbers to the nearest 10.

   a   183 _____   b   339 _____   c   495 _____

   d   303_____   e   245 _____   f   891 _____

2   Round each of these numbers to the nearest 100.

   a   183 _____   b   339 _____   c   495 _____

   d   303 _____   e   245 _____   f   891 _____

3   Mark this line with an arrow where you think each of these numbers lies.
   175   483   689

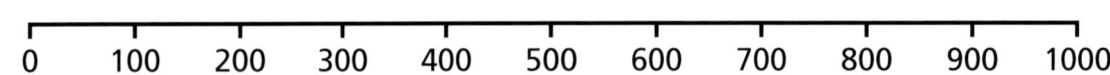

4   Estimate the number each arrow is pointing to.

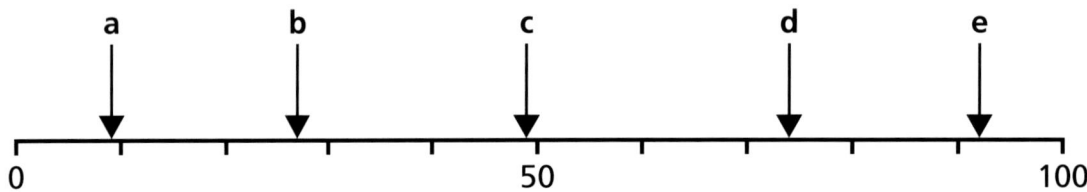

Train your brain!

Write all the whole numbers that round to 350 when rounded to the nearest 10. How many numbers are there?

How many whole numbers do you think round to 500 when rounded to the nearest 100?

What is the largest number? What is the smallest number?

I can round numbers to find approximate answers to calculations or problems.

Check-up scan 1D

Name: _____

1 Write the missing numbers on each number line.

a

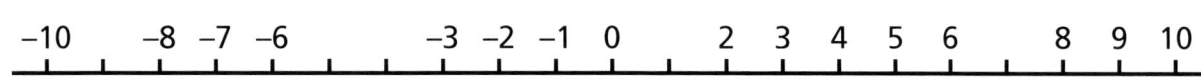

b

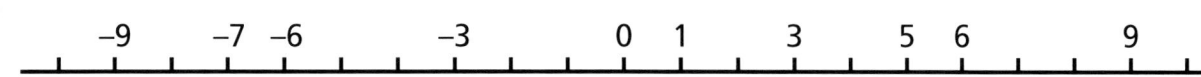

2 Circle the colder temperature in each pair.

    a 6 °C or –3 °C   **b** –4C or 0 °C

    c –2 °C or 3 °C   **d** –7 °C or –6 °C

    e –5 °C or –7 °C   **f** 0 °C or –8 °C

    g –5 °C or –6 °C   **h** –8 °C or 10 °C

3 Write these numbers in order of size starting with the smallest.

    a –2, –3, 4, 0, 5, –6   _____

    b –7, –6, 7, –4, 1, –2, 0   _____

    c 5, –4, 3, 6, –5, –2, –3   _____

Train your brain!

Find out the average temperatures in different parts of the world at different times of year. Can you find out temperatures in the North Pole, Antarctica, Russia, Iceland, Greenland or in the Scandinavian countries?

What is the coldest temperature you can find recorded?

I can order positive and negative numbers.

Check-up scan 1E

1 Write these amounts of money in pence.

   a £0.40 _____   **b** £0.69 _____   **c** £2.58 _____

2 Write these amounts of money in pounds.

   a 38p _____   **b** 47p _____   **c** 148p _____

3 How many 10p coins would you need to have £3.60? _____

4 Write these measurements in centimetres.

   a 1 m   _____   **b** 1.5 m   _____

   c 3.57 m _____

5 Write these measurements in metres.

   a 50 cm   _____   **b** 250 cm _____

   c 175 cm _____

6 A snail walks 2.8 m. How many centimetres is this? _____

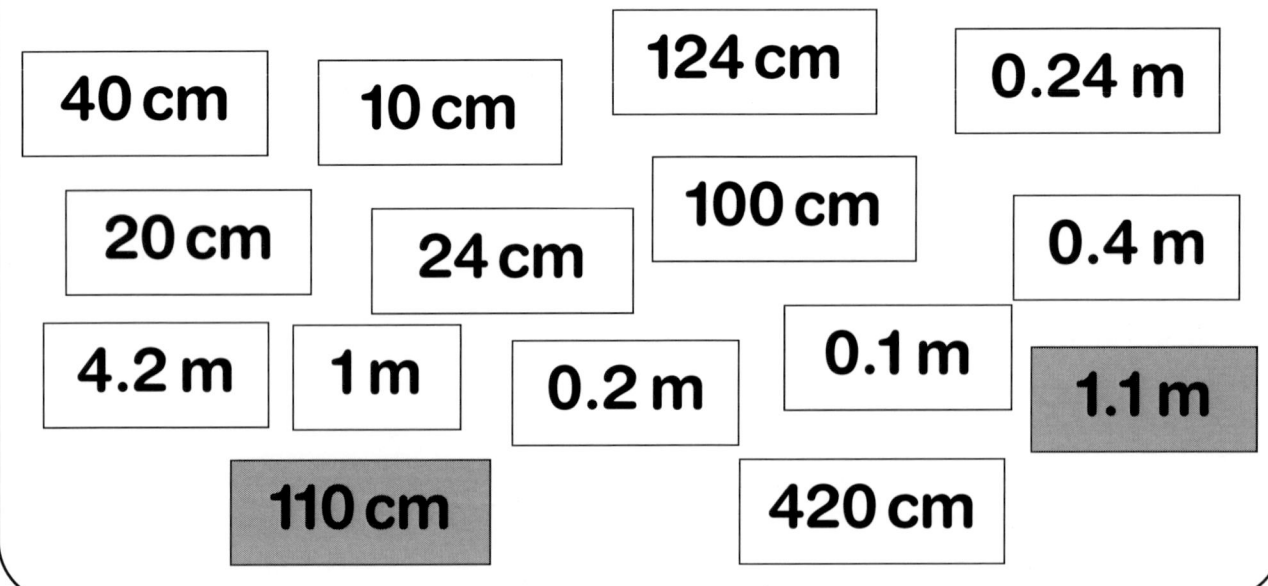

Train your brain!

Colour each pair of measurements that show the same length in a different colour.
One pair has been done for you.

40 cm   10 cm   124 cm   0.24 m
20 cm   24 cm   100 cm   0.4 m
4.2 m   1 m   0.2 m   0.1 m   1.1 m
110 cm   420 cm

I can solve problems that involve decimal numbers as money or measures.

Check-up scan 1F

Name: _____

1 What fraction of each shape is shaded?

a  _____

b 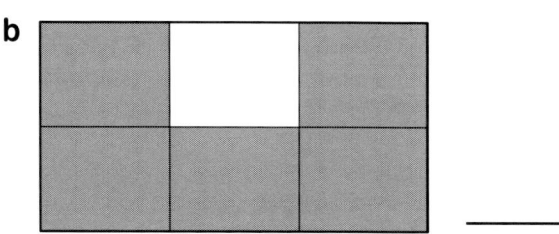 _____

c 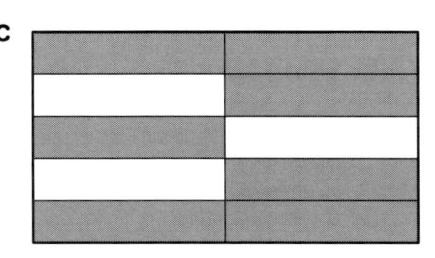 _____

d 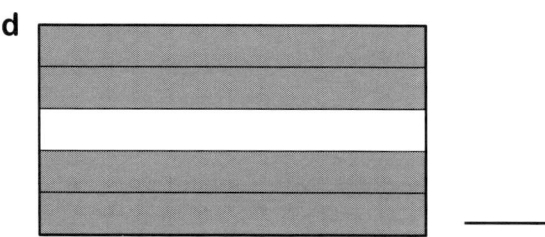 _____

e 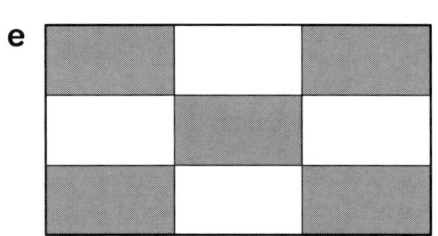 _____

f 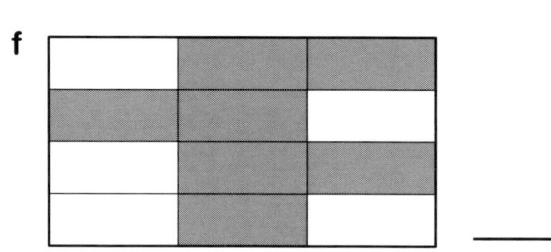 _____

2 What fraction of a metre is   a   47 cm?   b   50 cm?

3 What fraction of a pound is   a   99p?   b   25p?

Train your brain!

Use these digits to make four different fractions less than 1.
Make sure the numerator (top number) is smaller than the
denominator (bottom number).
Colour some of these shapes to show the fractions you have made.

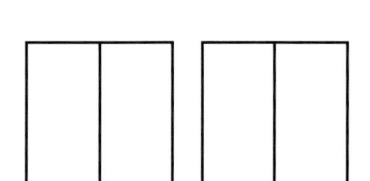 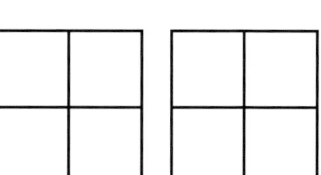 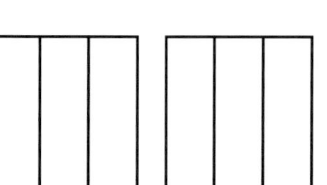

I can recognise and write a fraction of a shape.

© Rising Stars Ltd. 2010

Check-up scan 2A

1 Find the total for each row and column.

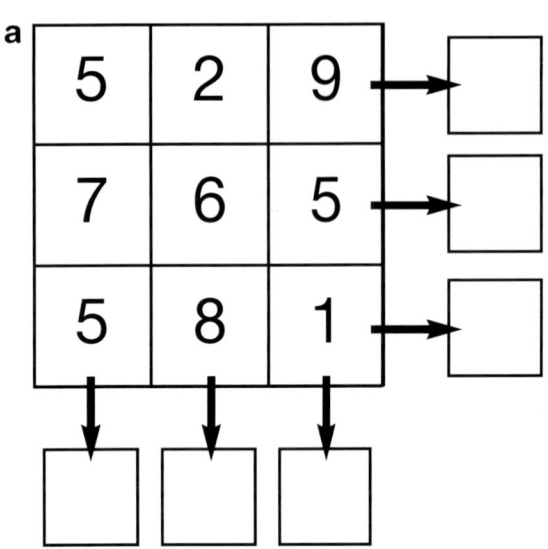

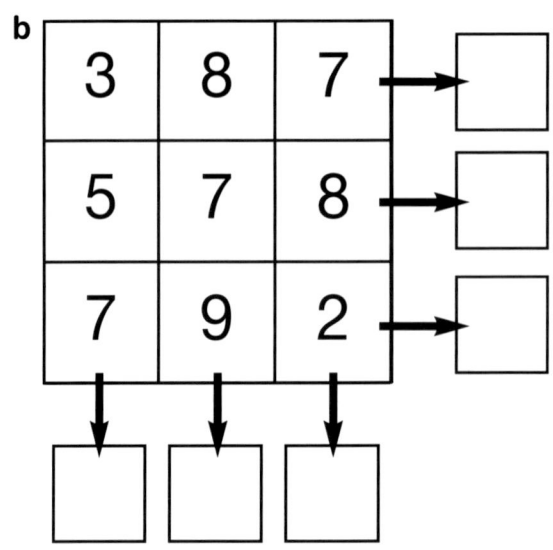

2 Write the answers to these questions.

    a $30 + 40 =$ _____   **b** $70 + 90 =$ _____   **c** $40 + 80 =$ _____

    d $130 - 80 =$ _____   **e** $140 - 90 =$ _____   **f** $110 - 80 =$ _____

3 Use the fact in the box to help you answer each of the other questions.

$$17 + 38 = 55$$

    a $55 - 38 =$ _____   **b** $17 + 58 =$ _____   **c** $170 + 380 =$ _____

    d $550 - 380 =$ _____   **e** $5500 - 1700 =$ _____   **f** $65 - 38 =$ _____

Train your brain!

$$36 + 47 = 83$$

Write four number facts that are related to this fact:

Choose two of the facts. For each, write a word problem that could be solved using it.

_____   _____

_____   _____

_____

I can add and subtract numbers using known facts.

Check-up scan 2B

Name: _____

1 Partition these numbers into tens and units. For example: 47 = 40 + 7

    a   39 =   **b**   28 =   **c**   74 =

2 Use partitioning to help you answer these questions.

    a   44 + 35   **b**   55 + 26   **c**   67 + 24

3   **a**   Write an addition fact to match the information on this number line.

b   Now write a related subtraction fact.

4 Use this number line to help you answer this question: 37 + 46 =

_____

Now check your answer using subtraction. Show your working.

Train your brain!

Use these digits to make four different additions and answer them.

8   **5**   **4**   **7**

☐☐ + ☐☐ =   ☐☐ + ☐☐ =

☐☐ + ☐☐ =   ☐☐ + ☐☐ =

I can add two-digit numbers, choosing an efficient method.   ☐

I can record the steps of my addition/subtraction methods.   ☐

I can check my answer to a calculation.   ☐

Check-up scan 2C

1   Tick the most sensible number sentence to match each problem.

   a   James bought a jacket that cost £11. He paid with a £20 note. How much change did he get?

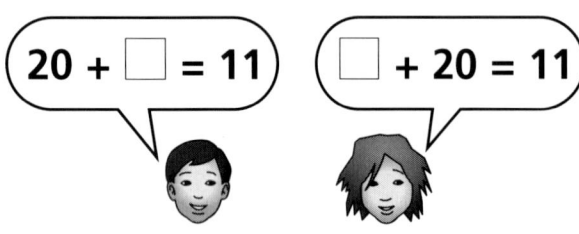 

$20 + \square = 11$ $\square + 20 = 11$ $20 - 11 = \square$ $11 - 20 = \square$

   b   Sam is 12 years older than Jude. Sam is 21, how old is Jude?

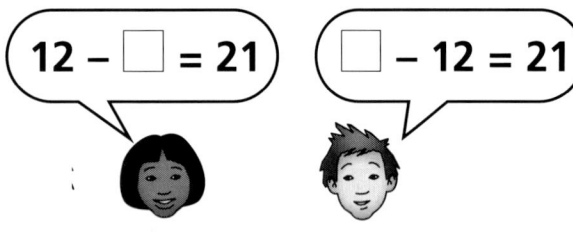 

$12 - \square = 21$ $\square - 12 = 21$ $21 - 12 = \square$ $21 - \square = \square$

2   Use a suitable method to find each missing number.

a $100 - \square = 47$	**b** $\square - 18 = 64$	**c** $\square + 67 = 100$
d $47 + \square = 100$	**e** $100 - 85 = \square$	**f** $\square - 38 = 47$

3   Write a number sentence to match this problem.

James has some money. He is given £38 more.
He now has £85. How much money did he
have at first?

Train your brain!

Write a story to match this missing-number sentence. $\_\_\_ + 52 = 90$

I can solve missing-number problems.   ☐

I can use addition and subtraction to solve problems.   ☐

Check-up scan 2D

Name: _____

1 Write a subtraction fact to match the information on each of these number lines.

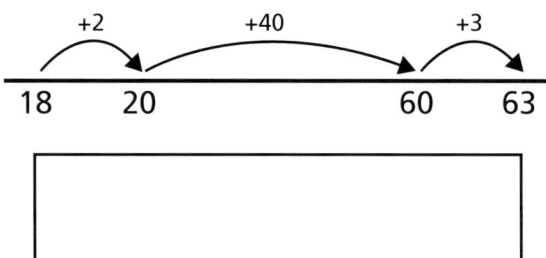

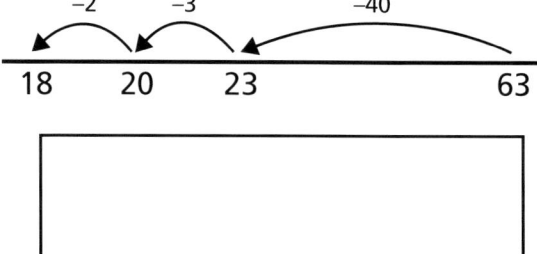

2 James wants to find the difference between 48 and 93.
Show one way that he could find the difference in the box .

3 Use a suitable method to help you answer these questions.

a 89 – 35   **b** 55 – 27   **c** 97 – 39

Train your brain!

Use these digits to make four different subtractions and answer them.

| 8 | 5 | 4 | 7 |

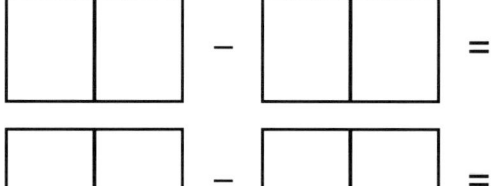

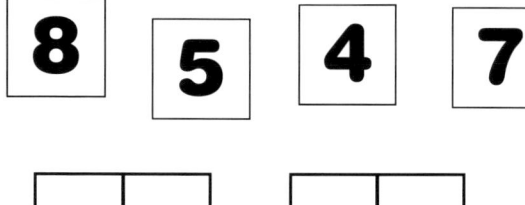

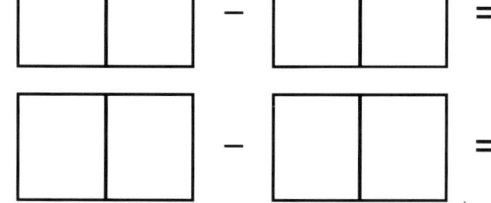

Make sure the first 2-digit number is larger than the second!

I can subtract one- and two-digit numbers, choosing an efficient method. ☐

I can record the steps of my subtraction methods. ☐

Check-up scan 3A

Name: _____

1   Write an addition and two multiplications for the number of spots on the ladybirds on each of these leaves.

a 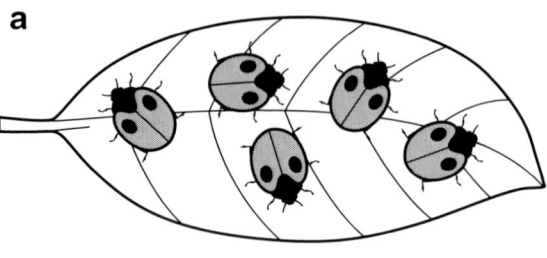   b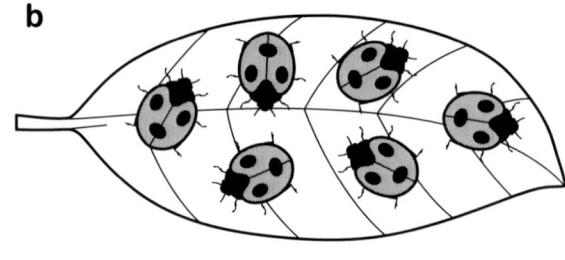

_____   _____

_____   _____

_____   _____

2   Write a multiplication to show how each of these additions could be written.

a   4 + 4 + 4 + 4 + 4 + 4 + 4 = 28 _____

b   6 + 6 + 6 + 6 + 6 = 30 _____

c   3 + 3 + 3 + 3 + 3 + 3 + 3 = 21 _____

3   Use the fact in the box to help you answer each of the questions.

$$5 \times 8 = 40$$

a   There are 8 chocolate bars in a pack. How many bars in 5 packs? ____

b   A school organises 40 children into 5 teams. How many children in each team? ____

c   A packet of crisps costs 40p. How much does it cost to buy 8 packets? ____

Train your brain!

$$\_\_ \times \_\_ = 24$$

Write as many multiplication facts with the answer 24 as you can.

I can show repeated addition as multiplication.   ☐

I can solve problems that involve multiplication.   ☐

1 Continue these sequences, counting back in equal steps.

a in 10s: 100 90 80 __ __ __ __ __ __ __ 0

b in 5:   50 45 40 __ __ __ __ __ __ __ 0

c in 3s: 30 27 24 __ __ __ __ __ __ __ 0

2 Work out each answer. Show how you worked it out.

a | 30 ÷ 5 =

b | 18 ÷ 3 =

c | 24 ÷ 4 =

d | 36 ÷ 6 =

3 Use the fact in the box to help you answer each of these questions.

$$6 \times 7 = 42$$

a 42 children are put into teams of 7. How many teams are there? _____

b Mrs Jones has £420. She shares the amount between her 6 children. How much do they each get? _____

c Seven people win £420 on the Lottery. They share it equally. How much do they each get? _____

d A coach can carry 60 children. How many coaches are needed to transport 420 children? _____

Train your brain!

Write two multiplication facts and a division fact that are related to this one.

$$24 ÷ 8 = 3$$

  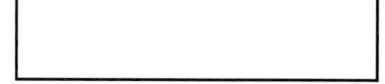

I can solve problems that involve division. ☐

Check-up scan 3C

1 Answer these multiplication questions.

a 5 × 5 =	**b** 4 × 3 =	**c** 3 × 5 =	**d** 7 × 3 =
e 4 × 10 =	**f** 5 × 0 =	**g** 6 × 3 =	**h** 1 × 8 =

2 Write two multiplication facts for each array.

a 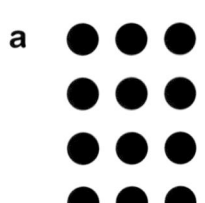   **b** 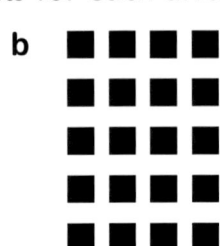   **c**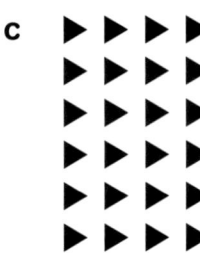

3 Use the diagram below to help you answer each question.

a 5 × 8 =   **b** 4 × 23 =

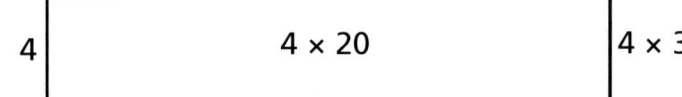

	10	8
5	5 × 10	5 × 8

	20	3
4	4 × 20	4 × 3

4 Work out 3 × 27. Show your working.

Train your brain!

Write two multiplication facts and a division fact that are related to this one.

$51 \div 3 = 17$

      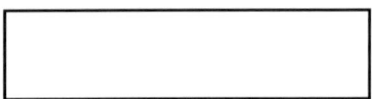

I can give the multiplication sentence that is linked to a division sentence and vice versa. ☐

I can multiply a two-digit by a one-digit number and record the steps I take. ☐

Check-up scan 3D

Name: _____

1   Each triangle tile has three numbers. Write two multiplication and two division facts using the numbers in each triangle.

a 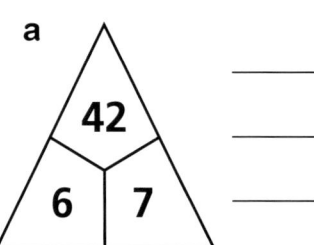   _____

_____

_____

_____

b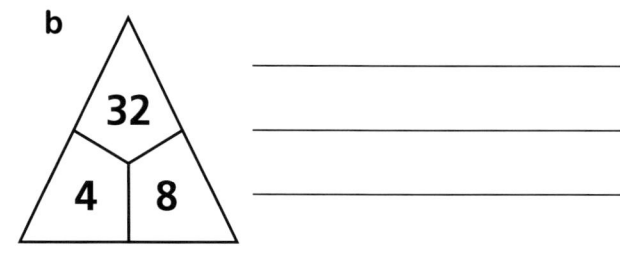

_____

_____

_____

_____

2   Use a chunking method to answer these questions.

   a 93 ÷ 4   **b** 71 ÷ 3   **c** 89 ÷ 4

3   **a**   How many 6p stamps can I buy with 86p?

   b   I need 59 envelopes. How many packs of 4 must I buy?

Train your brain!

Write a word problem using the numbers in this division question, but where the answer is 18.

$$52 \div 3 = 17 \text{ r}1$$

_____

_____

_____

I can give the multiplication sentence that is linked to a division sentence and vice versa. ☐

I can divide a two-digit by a one-digit number and record the steps I take. ☐

Check-up scan 3E

Name: _____

1 Write a division fact to show how each question could be answered.

    a What is $\frac{1}{7}$ of 14?

    b What is $\frac{1}{5}$ of 45?

    c What is $\frac{1}{8}$ of 40?

    d What is $\frac{1}{10}$ of 100?

2 Find these fractions of these amounts of money.

    a $\frac{1}{4}$ of £8 =

    b $\frac{1}{5}$ of £30 =

    c $\frac{1}{6}$ of £60 =

    d $\frac{2}{3}$ of £21 =

    e $\frac{7}{8}$ of £40 =

    f $\frac{3}{4}$ of £28 =

3 Write the answers to these questions and show your working.

    a There are 35 girls in a school. $\frac{2}{5}$ of them are wearing trousers. How many is this?

    b Of a group of 45 sheep, $\frac{2}{9}$ had grey faces. How many sheep had grey faces?

    c Of a group of 400 people at a football match, $\frac{7}{10}$ were men. How many were men?

Train your brain!

At a party there are boys and girls.

$\frac{5}{8}$ of the people at the party are girls.

There are 15 boys.

1 How many people are at the party altogether?

2 How many girls are there?

I can find fractions of amounts.

Check-up scan 4A

Name: _____

1 a Tick which of these shapes are hexagons.

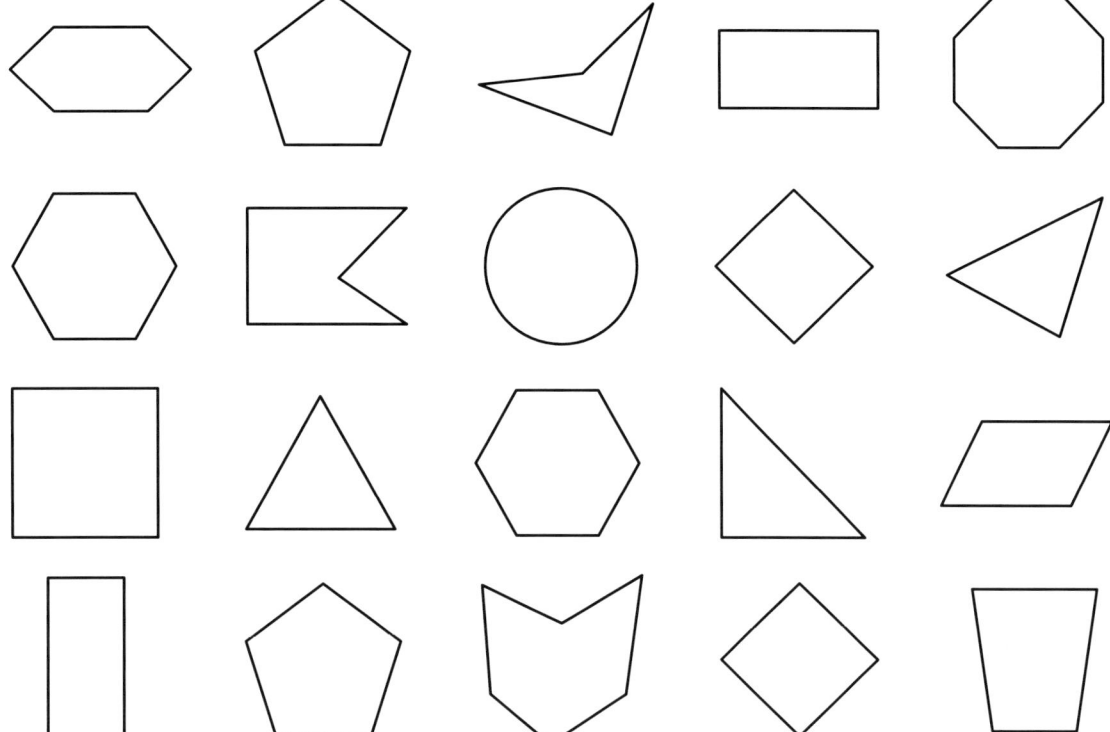

b With a red pencil, mark all the right angles you can see.

c Colour blue a pentagon that has no lines of symmetry.

2 Draw each of these shapes in the correct part of this Venn diagram.

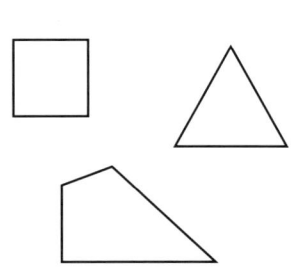
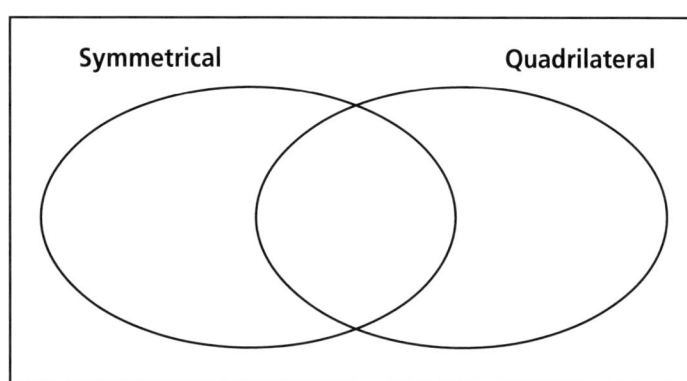

Train your brain!

Choose any shape from those above.
Write a description of it so that someone else can work out what it is.

I can sort 2-D shapes describing how I have classified them. ☐

I can identify whether shapes are symmetrical. ☐

© Rising Stars Ltd. 2010

Check-up scan 4B

Name: _____

1 You need some 3-D solid shapes. Think about where each shape would go in this diagram. Then write the names of the shapes in the correct places.

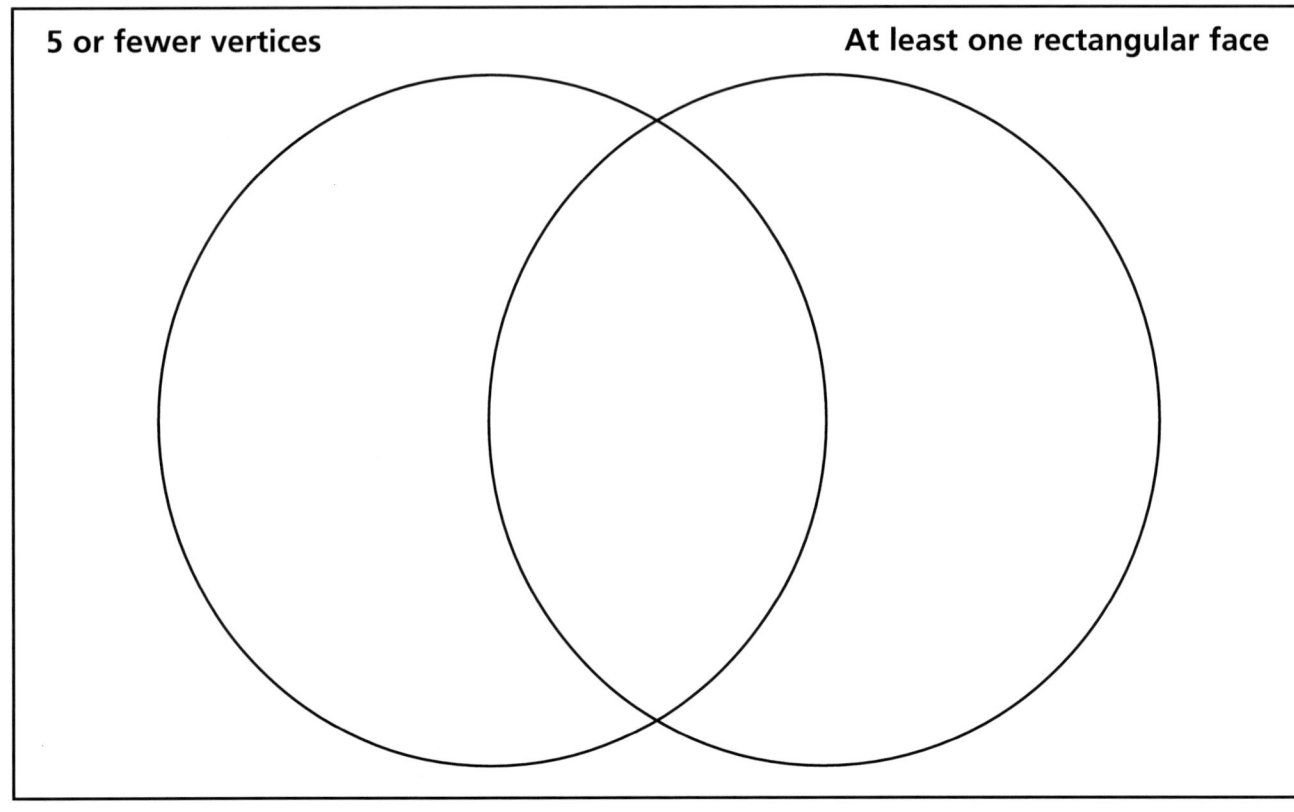

5 or fewer vertices

At least one rectangular face

2 What is the name of each shape being described here?

a It has one circular face and one curved face.
It has one vertex and one curved edge.

b It has two triangular faces and three rectangular faces.
It has 6 vertices and 9 edges.

Train your brain!

Choose any solid shape.
Write a description of it so that someone else could work out what it is.

I can sort 3-D shapes describing how I have classified them. ☐

I can visualise 3-D shapes. ☐

Check-up scan 4C

Name: _____

1 Draw shapes on the dotted grid to match each description.

Label each shape with its shape name.

a It has 3 sides and 1 right angle.

b It has 5 sides and 3 right angles.

c It has 6 sides and is symmetrical.

d It has 4 sides and no right angles.

2 You need some 3-D solid shapes. Think about where each shape would go in this diagram. Then write the names of the shapes into the correct places.

	At least one triangular face	No triangular faces
Prism		
Not a prism		

Train your brain!

Write a description of:　　**a** a cube　　**b** a cone　　**c** a cylinder

I can sort 3-D shapes and describe how I have classified them. ☐

I can draw shapes on a grid. ☐

I can visualise shapes. ☐

Check-up scan 4D

Name: _____

1 Write the letter of the shape that will continue each sequence.

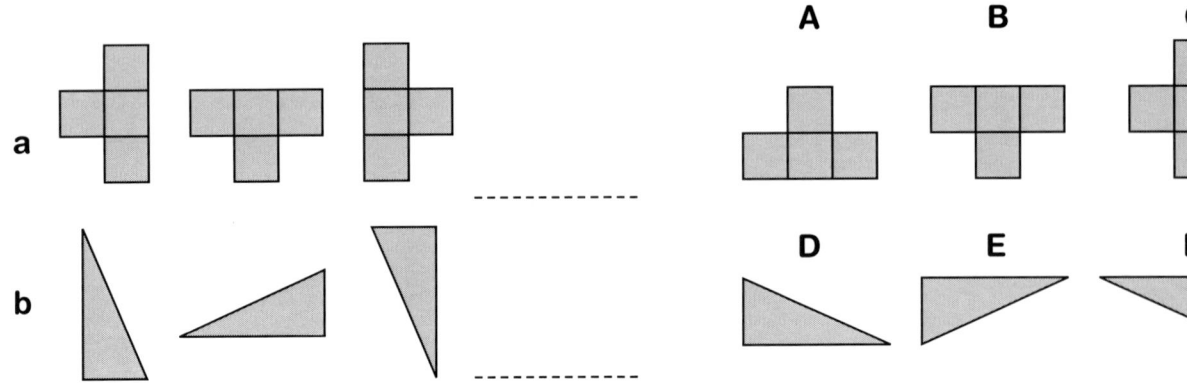

a _____

b _____

2 Draw a different pentagon in each box below.

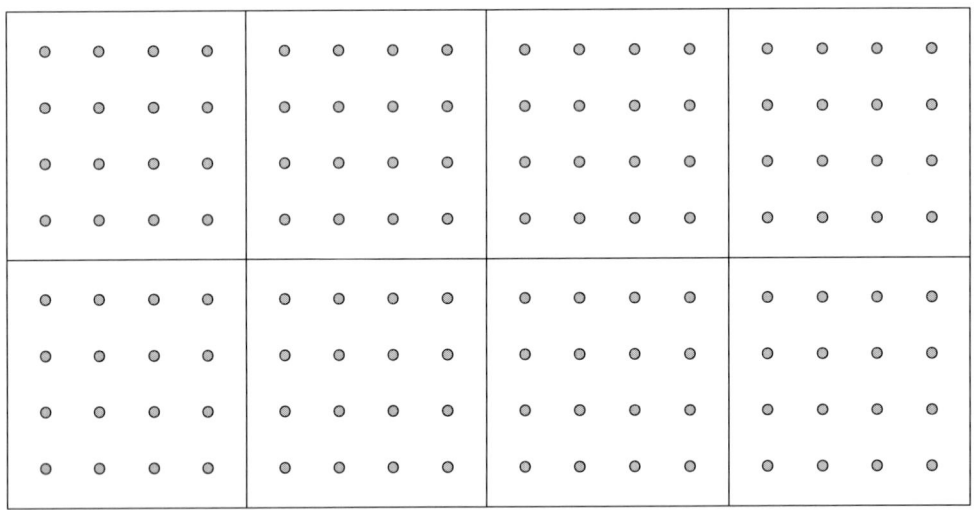

3 Tick which shape you think is the same shape as the shaded one.

 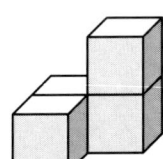 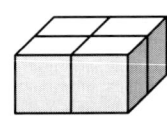 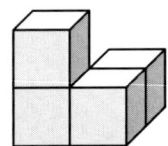 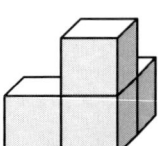

Train your brain!

Draw two shape sequences of your own like those in question 1.

Swap with a friend and work out the next shape in the sequence.

I can draw shapes on a grid. ☐

I can visualise shapes. ☐

Check-up scan 5A

Name: _____

1

£8 per large pizza   £6 per small pizza   £2 for each extra topping

Write a number sentence or sentences to show how you could find the cost of:

a 3 large pizzas and a small pizza   **b** 4 small pizzas

_____   _____

c a large pizza with 3 extra toppings   **d** 2 small pizzas, one of them with 2 extra toppings

_____   _____

2 Answer these questions and show what you did to work out each answer.

a My sister will be 20 in 4 years' time. I am half her age. How old am I?

b Mum had 24 cherry tomatoes. She ate 6 herself and shared the rest between her 6 children. How many did they each get?

c There are 12 tents and 4 caravans at a site. There are 2 people in each tent and 4 in each caravan. How many people?

Train your brain!

Write a word problem or story to match this number sentence.

$3 \times 4 + 1 = 13$

I can identify what operation(s) I need to do to solve a problem. ☐

I can jot down the steps to show how I worked out a problem. ☐

I can explain how I solved a problem. ☐

I can solve problems involving money. ☐

© Rising Stars Ltd. 2010

Check-up scan 5B

Name: _____

1 Fill in the missing numbers.

    a 1 metre = _____ centimetres   **b** 1 kilogram = _____ grams

    c 1 litre = _____ millilitres   **d** 1 kilometre = _____ metres

    e 4 kilograms = _____ grams   **f** $\frac{1}{2}$ kilogram = _____ grams

    g $\frac{1}{4}$ metre = _____ centimetres   **h** $\frac{1}{4}$ litre = _____ millilitres

2 Solve these problems. Show your working.

    a The total mass of these parcels is 2 kg. Two have the same mass and the larger one weighs 800 g. What is the mass of one of the smaller ones?

  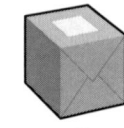

                          800g   ?   ?

    b Two identical containers together hold 900 ml. A smaller container holds 100 ml less than one of them. How much does it hold?

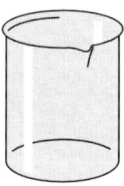 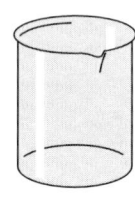 

    c A field is half as wide as it is long. It is 18 m wide. How long is it?

    d Two tables have a difference in length of 15 cm. The shorter table is 90 cm long. What is the length of the longer table?

Train your brain!

Write a word problem linking these three measurements: | 2 kg | 400 g | 1200 g |

I can identify what operation(s) I need to do to solve a problem. ☐

I can jot down the steps to show how I worked out a problem. ☐

I can explain how I solved a problem. ☐

I can solve problems that involve measures. ☐

Check-up scan 5C

Name: _____

1 Continue these time sequences.

a 3:00 3:05 3:10 ___ ___ ___ ___ ___ ___ 3:45

b 5:45 6:15 6:45 ___ ___ ___ ___ ___ ___ 10:15

c 3:15 3:25 3:35 ___ ___ ___ ___ ___ ___ 4:45

2 Use this diagram to find the time difference between 2:40 and 5:15.

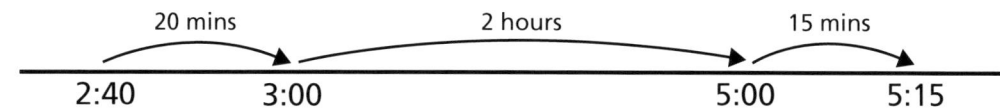

3 Draw your own diagram to help you find the difference between 4:45 and 7:10.

4 Answer these word problems.

a A TV show starts at 2:45. It lasts for $1\frac{3}{4}$ hours. What time does it end?

b Three-quarters of an hour ago, a TV show started at 5:25. What time is it now?

c A quarter of an hour ago, a TV show started at ten to five. What time is it now?

Train your brain!

Write three pairs of times with exactly $2\frac{3}{4}$ hours time difference.

I can solve problems that involve time.

☐

© Rising Stars Ltd. 2010

Check-up scan 6A

Name: _____

1   Look at this pictogram.

Types of bird that visited a bird table in 1 hour

Blackbird	
Robin	
Sparrow	
Magpie	
Greenfinch	= 2 birds

a   How many blackbirds were seen?   _____

b   How many greenfinches were seen?   _____

c   How many birds were seen altogether?   _____

d   Another 3 robins need to be added to the pictogram. Add these to the pictogram.

2   Look at this bar chart.

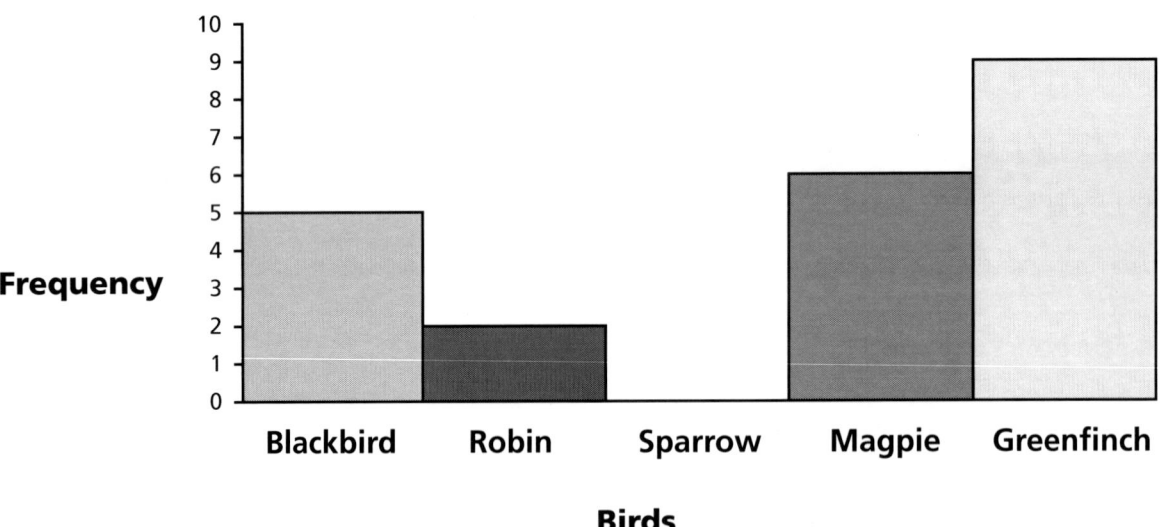

Types of bird that visited a bird table in 1 hour

Frequency (y-axis: 0 to 10)

Birds: Blackbird, Robin, Sparrow, Magpie, Greenfinch

Birds

This chart shows the same information as the pictogram but one of the bars is missing. Draw it on.

Train your brain!

Write three more facts about the information in the bar chart on the back of this sheet.

I can read information accurately from different sorts of graphs and charts.

Check-up scan 6B

Name: _____

1 Look at this table.

Children attending different school clubs each week

	Week 1	Week 2	Week 3
Art club	11	15	16
Netball club	16	16	14
Football club	11	12	12

a How many children went to art club in week 3? _____

b How many children went to football club in week 2? _____

c How many more children went to netball than art club in week 1? _____

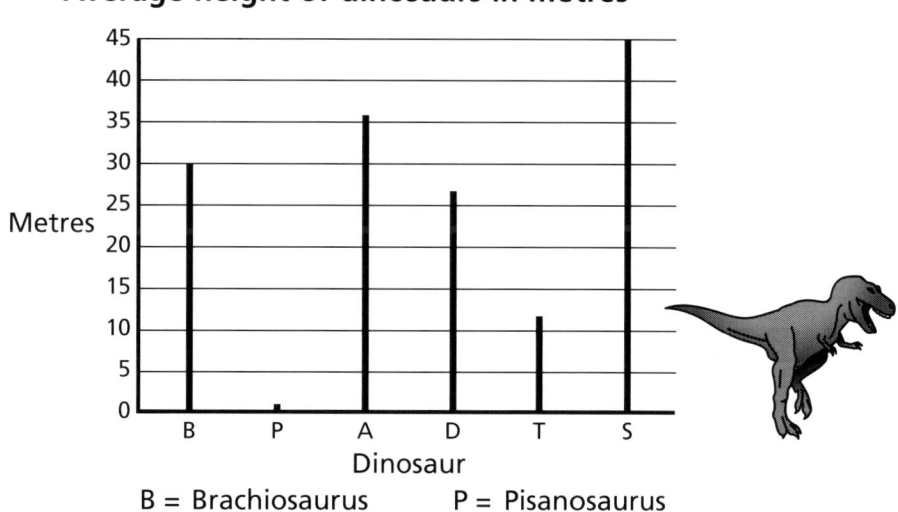

Average height of dinosaurs in metres

B = Brachiosaurus   P = Pisanosaurus
A = Argentinasaurus   D = Diplodocus
T = Tyrannosaurus   S = Seismosaurus

2 Approximately how tall was:

a a diplodocus? _____   **b** a brachiosaurus? _____

3 How much taller was an argentinasaurus than a tyrannosaurus? _____

Train your brain!

Write three more facts about the information on the chart above on the back of this sheet.

I can read information accurately from different sorts of graphs and charts. ☐

Check-up scan 6C

1 Write the number each arrow is pointing to.

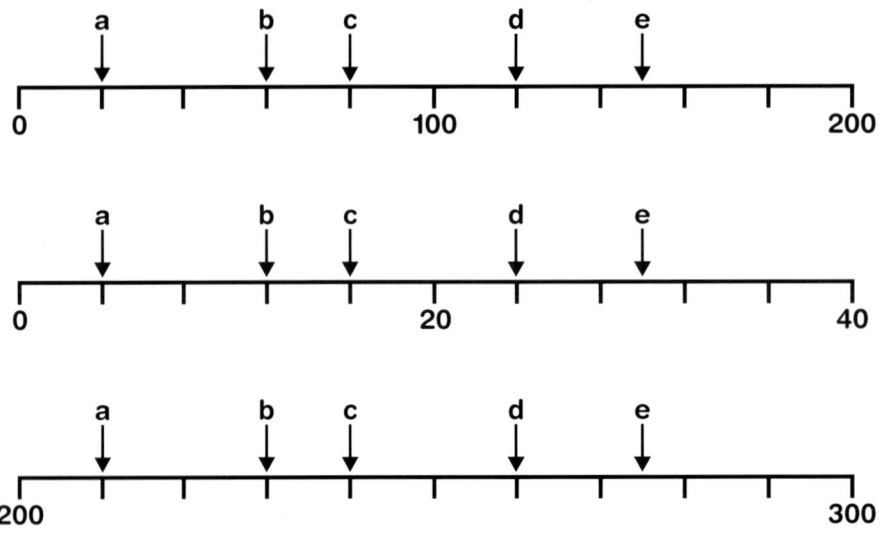

2 This bar-line graph shows the height of a male African elephant at different ages.

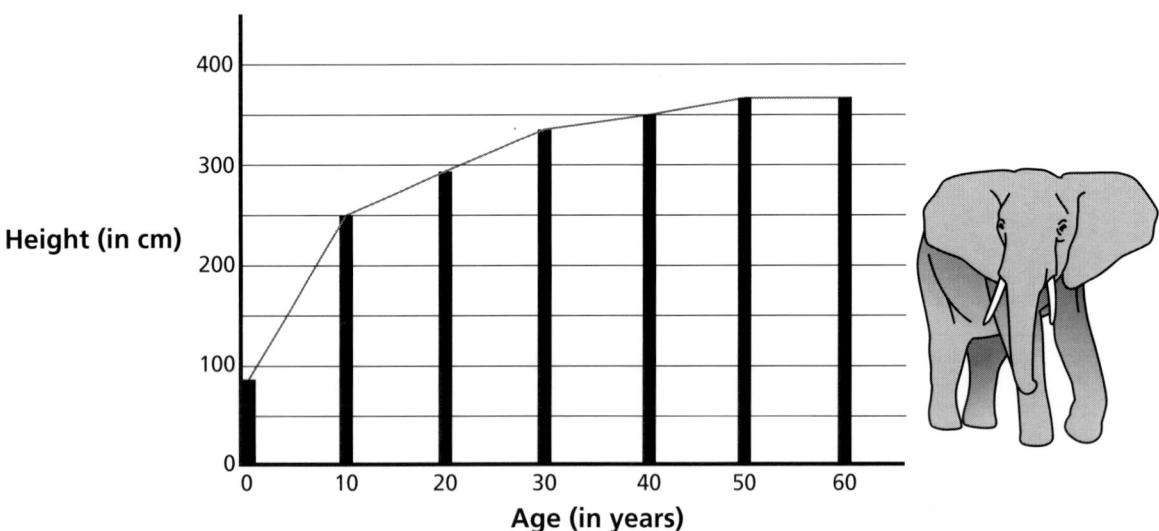

Approximately how tall is the elephant when he is:
a aged 40? _____   **b** aged 55? _____

Train your brain!

Estimate how tall the elephant is aged 25 and then aged 35.

I can interpret the scales along the axes of a graph to read data accurately. ☐

I can work out what information to use to answer a data-handling question. ☐

I can identify what calculations need to be done to answer a data-handling problem. ☐

Check-up scan 6D

Name: _____

1   What value lies exactly halfway between the two intervals on each scale below?

a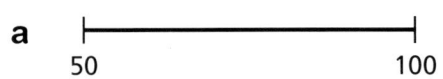
50   100

b
350   400

c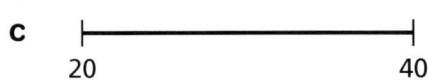
20   40

d
0   1000

2   What value lies exactly a quarter of the way between the two intervals on each scale below?

a
100   200

b
500   1000

c
200   400

d
50   150

3

Number of cans in a drinks machine during part of a day

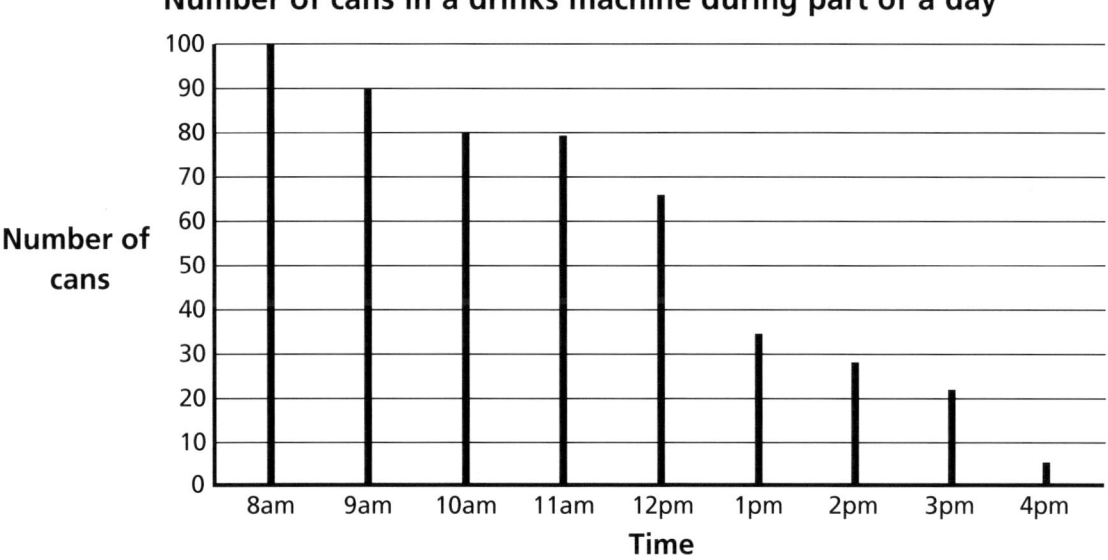

Number of cans

Time

a   How many cans were sold between 9am and 10am?
b   Between which two hours were the most cans sold?
c   About how many cans were sold between 12pm and 4pm?

Train your brain!

Write three more facts about the information on the chart above on the back of this sheet.

I can interpret the scales along the axes of a graph to read data accurately. ☐

I can work out what information to use to answer a data-handling question. ☐

I can identify what calculations need to be done to answer a data-handling problem. ☐

What I can do in mathematics   Name: _____

Unit 1
Understanding numbers

	:)	:|	:(
1a I understand the value of each digit in a three-digit number and can explain how I know			
1b I can multiply/divide a number by 10			
1c I can round numbers			
1d I can order negative and positive numbers			
1e I can solve problems that involve decimal numbers as money or measures			
1f I can recognise and write a fraction of a shape			

What I can do in mathematics   Name: _____

Unit 2
Mental addition and subtraction

	:)	:|	:(
2a I can add and subtract numbers using known facts			
2b I can add two-digit numbers, choosing an efficient method			
2b I can record the steps of my addition/subtraction methods			
2b I can check my answer to a calculation			
2c I can solve missing number problems			
2c I can use addition and subtraction to solve problems			
2d I can subtract one- and two-digit numbers, choosing an efficient method			
2d I can record the steps of my subtraction methods			

Unit 4
Understanding of shapes

	😊	😐	🙁
4a I can sort shapes describing how I have classified them			
4a I can identify whether shapes are symmetrical			
4b I can sort shapes describing how I have classified them			
4b I can visualise shapes			
4c I can sort shapes describing how I have classified them			
4c I can draw shapes on a grid			
4c I can visualise shapes			
4d I can draw shapes on a grid			
4d I can visualise shapes			

© Rising Stars Ltd. 2010   Shine!/Level 3

Unit 3
Understanding multiplication and division

	😊	😐	🙁
3a I can show repeated addition as multiplication			
3a I can solve problems that involve multiplication			
3b I can solve problems that involve division			
3c I can give the multiplication sentence that is linked to a division sentence and vice versa			
3c I can multiply a two-digit by a one-digit number and record the steps I take			
3d I can give the multiplication sentence that is linked to a division sentence and vice versa			
3d I can divide a two-digit by a one-digit number and record the steps I take			
3e I can find fractions of amounts			

© Rising Stars Ltd. 2010   Shine!/Level 3

Unit 5
Problem solving using money and measures

		☺	😐	☹
5a	I can identify what operation(s) I need to do to solve a problem			
5a	I can jot down the steps to show how I worked out a problem			
5a	I can explain how I solved a problem			
5a	I can solve problems involving money			
5b	I can identify what operation(s) I need to do to solve a problem			
5b	I can jot down the steps to show how I worked out a problem			
5b	I can explain how I solved a problem			
5b	I can solve problems that involve measures			
5c	I can solve problems that involve time			

Unit 6
Problem solving using tables and graphs

		☺	😐	☹
6a	I can read information accurately from different sorts of graphs and charts			
6b	I can read information accurately from different sorts of graphs and charts			
6b	I can add or subtract numbers using known facts			
6c	I can interpret the scales along the axes of a graph to read data accurately			
6c	I can work out what information to use to answer a data-handling question			
6c	I can identify what calculations need to be done to answer a data-handling problem			
6d	I can interpret the scales along the axes of a graph to read data accurately			
6d	I can work out what information to use to answer a data-handling question			
6d	I can identify what calculations need to be done to answer a data-handling problem			